Advent in Plain Sight

A Devotion through Ten Objects

JILL J. DUFFIELD

D1302177

WESTMINSTER
JOHN KNOX PRESS
LOUISVILLE • KENTUCKY

First Edition
Published by Westminster John Knox Press
Louisville, Kentucky

21 22 23 24 25 26 27 28 29 30—10 9 8 7 6 5 4 3 2 1

Book design by Sharon Adams
Cover design by Allison Taylor

Library of Congress Cataloging-in-Publication Data
Names: Duffield, Jill J., author.
Title: Advent in plain sight : a devotion through ten objects / Jill J. Duffield.
Description: First edition. | Louisville, Kentucky : Westminster John Knox Press, 2021. | Summary: "In this daily devotional for Advent, Christmas, and Epiphany, Jill J. Duffield draws readers' attention to ten ordinary objects that appear in the biblical narratives of messianic prophesy and incarnation. Through these objects, readers will find new meaning in the biblical account of Jesus' coming"-- Provided by publisher.
Identifiers: LCCN 2021013911 (print) | LCCN 2021013912 (ebook) | ISBN 9780664267148 (paperback) | ISBN 9781646982035 (ebook)
Subjects: LCSH: Advent--Prayers and devotions. | Christmas--Prayers and devotions.
Classification: LCC BV40 .D835 2021 (print) | LCC BV40 (ebook) | DDC 242/.33--dc23
LC record available at https://lccn.loc.gov/2021013911
LC ebook record available at https://lccn.loc.gov/2021013912

Most Westminster John Knox Press books are available at special quantity discounts when purchased in bulk by corporations, organizations, and special-interest groups. For more information, please e-mail SpecialSales@wjkbooks.com.

To Grant with gratitude and love

Contents

Introduction

Advent, that liturgical season marked by eager waiting, often brings with it a frenzy of busyness. Cultural expectations around Christmas invade our church Advent rituals. Getting overwhelmed by events and activities tempts us to forget that we are, in fact, preparing for both Jesus' birth and Christ's return. We lose sight of the holy in our midst, distracted by commercialism or an unexamined sense of what the season is supposed to entail. Imagine if instead disciples of Jesus Christ entered Advent with a hope and anticipation of seeing the divine at work all around and within us. Imagine if Christians took Advent as an invitation to slow down, rather than speed up, to ponder instead of purchase, to look for God in all things even as we wait for the Word made flesh to appear.

Having the eyes to see and the ears to hear the holy in the middle of daily demands and anxiety-provoking times takes an openness to the work of the Holy Spirit. This book is a prayerful attempt to invite readers to an intentional perspective that seeks to see God in all things in the hope of discerning divine possibility in what at first glance appears to be utterly mundane. Scripture bears witness to the fact that our God chooses to work through all creation, through worldly, unnoteworthy things and people. Moses hears God's voice in a burning bush. Balaam's donkey speaks. Jesus says that if people keep silent, the rocks will cry out. A star guides the magi and on-duty shepherds are the first to get word of the Messiah's birth.

Could this be the Advent we remember Immanuel, God with us, in all places, reminded of God's presence, providence, and power by everyday objects that point us to the salvation story of which we are a part? Being mindful of the divine in the midst of our living takes intentionality and focus; each section of this book encourages readers to pay attention to a particular object, allowing that tangible item to point to the sometimes ineffable work of God in our lives and world. Noticing the everyday things we encounter as we go about our day and connecting them to Scripture and the triune God, we become aware of Immanuel, God with us, past, present, and future.

May this Advent season be one where your anticipation of Jesus' birth and your expectation of Christ's return allow you to see God in all things and at all times. My prayer is that this book helps you feel surrounded by the love of the One who came to save the world.

Jill Duffield
October 2020

First Week of Advent

Gates

Sunday

Genesis 28:1–5, 10–22

And he was afraid, and said, "How awesome is this place! This is none other than the house of God, and this is the gate of heaven."

Genesis 28:17

Gates of Heaven

Jacob sets out on a journey at the behest of his father: Go to your mother's father and take a wife, a wife from within the family, a wife who is a member of and approved by your people. Isaac blesses his son Jacob, and Jacob obediently sets out on his way toward Haran. He stops for the night, finds a stone for a pillow, and settles in to sleep only to have his slumber disrupted by a vivid dream of a ladder bridging the divide between heaven and earth. Angels come and go, up and down, but then the Lord comes and stands right beside Jacob, the divide between holy and human virtually nonexistent. God's words echo Isaac's, another comingling of divine and secular. Isaac asks God to make Jacob "a company of peoples" and grant him the land God gave to Abraham. God seems to have heard Isaac's prayer but goes a lot further, saying Jacob will indeed possess the land, but he will not only be a company of peoples, he and his offspring will be the means through which God will bless all companies of people. Further, God will keep Jacob throughout the entire journey. No wonder Jacob wakes up fearful and exuberant, declaring, "How awesome is this place! This is none other than the house of God, and this is the gate of heaven."

This is not just a "thin place" where the barrier between God and humans is nominal, this is a place where the gate to the heavenly kingdom has been flung open wide and the Lord God has walked through it and come for a night visit. God, in this story, sits at Jacob's bedside. Imagine God coming into your room in the middle of the night, sitting beside you, and giving you such a mind-blowing word. *You* will be the conduit for my blessing not just to your family or your community or your people but to no less than everyone in all creation. When God chooses to open the gate to our hearts and heads and homes and walk through, the flood gates of divine blessings open too.

In Ephesians 3:20, we read that Christ's "power at work within us is able to accomplish abundantly far more than all we can ask or imagine." The ultimate opening of the gates of heaven, of God come to earth, the incarnation, continues God's promise of blessedness and blessing. As we prepare for the birth of Jesus and the return of Christ, all around us God opens the gates of heaven, breaches whatever barriers we erect, puts in place not just ladders between the divine and the dailiness of our lives, but comes and sits beside us, blessing us and making of us a blessing, not to just a company of peoples, but to all the families of the earth. This Advent we can trust God's promise never to leave us and to accomplish more than we can ask or imagine through us because with Christ's coming, no matter where we are is no less than the gate of heaven.

Questions for Reflection

1. As you enter this season of Advent, where do you sense God's close presence? How can you invite an awareness of God with you wherever you are?
2. Where do you encounter gates? What are they keeping in or keeping out? What is their purpose? When you see a gate this week, imagine God breaching it and seeking out those on the other side of it. Imagine what God might say to those on either side of the gate.
3. How is it that you are blessed in order to be a blessing to all the families of the earth?

Prayer for the Day

Lord who knows no bounds and whose blessing is for all the families of the earth, we too often truncate your expansive grace, basking in your care for us without extending your compassion to others. Forgive our limited vision and diminished imagination. As we prepare for Christ's coming, we yearn for hearts to welcome him, hands to point to him, mouths to speak of him, and minds that are conformed to him. Open our eyes to see your angels all around us. Visit us in our vulnerability and open any gate that seeks to keep you at bay from any aspect of our lives. Amen.

Monday

Keep these words that I am commanding you today in your heart. Recite them to your children and talk about them when you are at home and when you are away, when you lie down and when you rise. Bind them as a sign on your hand, fix them as an emblem on your forehead, and write them on the doorposts of your house and on your gates.

Deuteronomy 6:6–9

Your Gates

Focus. Paying attention. Taking notice. How elusive are such qualities in our culture and in our lives? How easily are we distracted by many things? The ping of a text, the pull of our social media accounts, the to-do list constantly running in our minds? My prayer as of late has been only this: Lord, what do you want me to notice today? Simplistic, I suppose, and yet difficult to do even with the best of intentions. So prone am I to distraction and fixating on the trivial or negative that I have taped an Annie Dillard quote to my desk, visible to me as I work. In her book *The Writing Life*, she says, "How we spend our days is, of course, how we spend our lives. What we do with this hour, and that one, is what we are doing."* Where we direct our attention is often where we put our energy and subsequently how we spend our lives. God seems to understand this aspect of our human finitude, giving the Israelites very specific instructions on not only where to focus, but hacks for how to sustain it.

God tells God's people to love the Lord with all their heart, soul, and might. We know this commandment and the one like unto it: to love our neighbors as ourselves. In Judaism, Deuteronomy 6:4–9 is known as the Shema, the oldest fixed prayer in Judaism, recited in the morning and the evening, "when you lie down and when you rise." God explicitly tells God's people that their focus should be on God, intently, completely, always on God. Recite this truth, but also write this truth, affix it on your person and on your property. Use tefillin or phylacteries for the body and a mezuzah for your door. Keep focus. On God. Always.

As we begin our Advent journey, where is our focus? On whom or what are we fixated? If we are not attentive to loving God with all our heart, soul, and might, all of our other priorities will be disordered. Mezuzah means "doorpost" and observant Jews place within these small containers the Shema (Deut. 6:4–9, 11:13–21) and affix them to the doorframe of their homes—a visible and tangible reminder of where, and on whom, to focus. As we come and go this Advent season, crossing countless thresholds, could we allow those "gates" to remind us to focus? Every time we come in or go out of a room or a

---

*Annie Dillard, *The Writing Life* (New York: Harper & Row, 1989), 32.

building, could those entries and exits give us pause and invite us to pray to love the Lord our God with all our heart, soul, and might—and our neighbors as ourselves? Our focus on our love for our Lord will surely open the gates of our compassion for everyone we encounter on the other side of those doorways. Our intentional focus on the Lord will help us to let go of many distractions and enable us to see all that God wants us to notice today, enable us to live our days and our lives in ways that are pleasing in God's sight.

Questions for Reflection

1. Where do you find your focus fixating? What do you fail to see as a result?
2. What are the "gates," the thresholds you cross every day? What do you want to notice on the other side of them?
3. Are there particular Bible verses you might write down and affix to a place you will see daily to help remind you where, and on whom, to focus?

Prayer for the Day

Lord God, our attention wanders and we often find ourselves focused on ourselves or the faults of others or on the trivial, anything but your glory and grace. We easily forget that you are the center of our lives and creator of all that is, seen and unseen. As we prepare for Christ's coming, call us back to the one thing we truly have need of: You. As we come and go this day remind us of your presence and your providence that we might worship you, love you, with all our heart, soul, and might, and see all the beauty and truth you reveal to us as a result. Amen.

Tuesday

Psalm 118

Open to me the gates of righteousness, that I may enter through them and give thanks to the LORD.

Psalm 118:19

Gates of Righteousness

The Lord's steadfast love endures forever, so goes the refrain of this Psalm of victory. The proclamation of the Lord's steadfast love begins and ends this hymn and is repeated three times in between. The thread woven through recollections of perilous circumstances and real and present threats is the Lord's steadfast love. Somehow the psalmist still sees the love of God even when "severely punished." Of course, this confident cry comes in hindsight, after the victory is won and the people are set in a broad, safe place. One wonders what the writer called out to God when the battle raged and escape appeared all but impossible.

Søren Kierkegaard wrote, "Life can only be understood backwards; but it must be lived forwards." Hence, that oft repeated idiom, hindsight is 20/20. We walk through most of life's gates without much knowledge of what lies on the other side of them, not really. We marry and bring children in the world without any way of knowing the detailed ramifications of those decisions. We move or choose or are forced to change jobs. We speak or write a word only to discover after it is let loose in the universe its implications and reception. It is all well and good to sing of God's steadfast love and salvation after we land on the other side of a sickness or divorce or pandemic or lay-off, but what about when we are smack dab in the middle of life's upheavals?

Psalm 118, verse 24, is surely one of the most familiar of verses in the Bible, "This is the day that the LORD has made, let us rejoice and be glad in it." The unequivocal nature of this statement challenges us to declare it regardless of present circumstance. This day, whatever it holds, whatever we encounter within whatever walls we find ourselves, is, in fact, a day that the Lord has made, we will rejoice and be glad in it. This day, no matter the content of it, is permeated and bookended by the Lord's steadfast love. Living in this truth and promise prompts us to praise God and creates the gates of righteousness in every place and time.

Remember, however, the middle of this psalm of victory, the angry, uncomfortable part, verses that contain words like "distress" and being "surrounded on every side." Sentiments like being "pushed hard" and "punished severely." Those singing this psalm rejoice from a place of deep pain. Perhaps that is what makes the song resonate through the ages, particularly in the season of Advent, when joy is bittersweet for those who are mourning or depressed. Those entering the gates of righteousness in order to give thanks to God know in the marrow of their bones a hard-won gratitude that comes steeped in real loss. The thanks we give to our steadfast loving, saving God is not cheap gratitude. Our declarations of praise well up from the pure relief of having been brought back to life from a near-death experience we will never forget. The humbled and relieved, those who know lament and despair, enter the gates of righteousness with uncontainable joy and shouts of gladness, a backwards understanding that propels them forward in faith.

Questions for Reflection:

1. What experiences have you lived through that you now understand in hindsight? How does this "backwards understanding" help you understand your present reality?
2. Have there been times in your life when you have entered the "gates of righteousness" and given thanks to God?
3. As you prepare for Christ's coming, for what do you give God thanks?

Prayer for the Day

Lord, your steadfast love endures forever. Your love for us and for all creation is the alpha and the omega, the beginning, end, and middle of the world. As we face challenges and change, uncertainties and unwelcome experiences, open our eyes to see your steadfast love within them all. Open to us the gates of righteousness, that we may enter them and give you thanks. This is the day that the Lord has made, let us rejoice and be glad in it, no matter what it brings. This is the day that the Lord has made, we will rejoice and be glad in it because the Lord is our strength and might. Amen.

Wednesday

Jeremiah 7:1–7

*Stand in the gate of the LORD's house, and proclaim
there this word, and say, Hear the word of the LORD,
all you people of Judah, you that enter these gates to
worship the LORD.*

Jeremiah 7:2

The Gate of the Lord's House

The Lord instructs Jeremiah what to say and where to say
it. Jeremiah's proclamation of God's word resounds from
the gate of the Lord's house throughout the city and that
word requires a response. Jeremiah's sermon is no mere
"FYI" or interesting trivia. The word of the Lord coming
from the threshold of the Lord's house stops listeners in
their tracks and demands change. "Amend your ways."
Change your practices. Alter your actions. Those who
wish to enter the gates of the Lord's house must behave
in ways commensurate with the character of the owner.
Crossing the boundary into God's temple should not be

done casually or without consenting to act in accordance with God's commandments.

Amend your ways, the prophet calls from the gates. Truly amend your ways and your deeds, Jeremiah repeats lest his listeners miss the message. The expectations of those who enter the gates of the Lord and reside within the gates of this godly community include justice for all people, care for the vulnerable and refraining from violence. Would that we did not still need to hear Jeremiah's recitation of the Lord's commands. Would that we did not still enter the doors of our places of worship without carefully considering if our lives reflect the character and commandments of the One we worship.

Jeremiah's sermon still preaches and those of us preparing for the incarnation ought to listen carefully, lest we think we can welcome Jesus Christ without honestly amending our ways and our deeds. As God readies to cross the threshold from heaven to earth, we who anticipate Jesus' coming lean into Jeremiah's urgent word to change. To make amends. To respond to the Word of the Lord with actions that reflect God's love for the world and demand for justice. Advent demands more from us than lighting candles and decorating our sanctuaries. Advent requires that we truly change the way we live. Every time we enter the gates of the Lord's house we ought to ask ourselves if our deeds match our doctrine, our actions reflect God's attitudes to the most vulnerable and our ways echo the divine Word. Jeremiah reminds us to never walk through the Lord's gates without taking seriously what the Lord requires of the worshipers therein.

Amend your ways. Prepare not only for the birth of Jesus, but for the return of Christ. Truly act justly with one another. Do not oppress the alien, the orphan, or the widow. Do not shed innocent blood. Do not go after other gods. Then, the Lord says, "I will dwell with you in this place." Are we ready, then, to enter the Lord's gates, given these requirements for admittance? If not, Jeremiah stands at the gate of the Lord's house and declares to all those within the bounds of our cities and towns, "Truly amend your ways and your doings."

Questions for Reflection

1. Do you consider if your ways and deeds align with the commandments of the Lord before you enter God's house to worship? This week, when you go to worship, think about this as you enter and leave the church building.
2. How and with whom do you need to make amends? Can you begin to do so this week?
3. In your church and community, what historic and systemic oppression do you need to address, truly and tangibly? How is that amends being made?

Prayer for the Day

Lord, your prophet's painful word resounds through the ages. We still worship without carefully considering if our lives and deeds reflect your commands and character. We act as if entering the gates of your home requires nothing, let alone all our heart, soul, mind, and strength. We recognize the incongruity between our ways and yours. We ask now to truly make amends. Take our desire to conform to your will and transform that desire into real change that brings justice, compassion, and peace for all your children, especially those long exploited, those scared and vulnerable, and those most in need of relief. Amen.

Thursday

Matthew 24:29–35

"From the fig tree learn its lesson: as soon as its branch becomes tender and puts forth its leaves, you know that summer is near. So also, when you see all these things, you know that he is near, at the very gates."

Matthew 24:32–33

At the Very Gates

I remember sitting on the second-hand sofa of an Episcopal campus ministry center when the priest asked those of us gathered what we thought about when we thought about Advent. This community of faith drew not just students but recent grads like me and my husband, a few faculty from the nearby university, and an assortment of people who lived in the neighborhood. Our small but diverse group was eclectic, thoughtful, and open-minded. We responded to our fearless leader's query. Advent is that season where we prepare for the incarnation, the coming of Jesus to earth, the breaking of barriers between heaven and earth. I am sure the word "Immanuel" got tossed around as we talked of God with us.

The priest listened and then said with exasperation, "No one ever thinks of the Second Coming!" I suspect part of his irritation stemmed from the fact he had been preaching the lectionary texts on just that theme for several weeks. Texts like this one from Matthew about Christ's return, the sun and moon going dark, and the need to make ready not only for sweet, baby Jesus, but for justice-bringing, sheep-and-goat-sorting, risen and returning Christ. The latter is a tougher sell in this season of twinkling lights and "Here Comes Santa Claus." All the more important then that disciples prepare not only for the birth of Jesus, but for Christ's return.

What would it mean for our daily living, the choices we make, the lens through which we see the world, if we considered the fig tree and wondered if, in fact, Jesus Christ is as near as the gates through which we pass daily? Our front door? The city limits of our town? The border of our country? What if the risen Christ returned and showed up at one of the many barriers we erect to keep those we consider insiders safe and those we consider outsiders at bay?

Jesus' birth gets announced by the angels as good news of great joy for all people, not some people or a few people, but all people. The returning Christ judges all the nations. John's Gospel proclaims that the Word became flesh to save the world, as a light to the cosmos. As we get ready to welcome the infant born to Mary in the stable, God with us, we are also called to remember to be on the lookout for the returning, victorious, Christ, God who judges all. Such awareness ought not engender fear, but certainly should cause us to pause at every gate we cross and ask ourselves what it would mean to meet the risen Christ there and do an audit of our discipleship with him. As we see the decorations go up in storefronts and the jaunty Christmas classics take over the cultural soundtrack, we who mark the season of Advent might consider them a fig tree like sign reminding us to be on watch for the return of the One who says we will be judged based upon how we treated the hungry, the prisoner, the poor, the most vulnerable among us, those we often ignore at our very gates, the very gates where Christ is right now present, if we are willing to see him there.

Questions for Reflection

1. When you think of the season of Advent, what do you think about? Do you prepare for the birth of Jesus and also for Christ's return?
2. What do you make of texts like this one from Matthew, apocalyptic texts, that talk of cosmic and earthly upheaval? How is this good news?
3. If Christ were to return today, if you met Christ at one of the thresholds you cross daily, what conversation would you have with him?

Prayer for the Day

God of all that is seen and unseen, as we prepare for the birth of Jesus this Advent, remind us also to make ready personally and corporately for the return of Christ. Help us to see those on the margins, those often on the other side of locked gates, as Christ himself. Do not let us conflate the great gift of Immanuel, God with us, as somehow God on our side or God with us, but not with others. May the truth that Jesus came to save the world enliven our compassion for all creation and every living being within it. Amen.

Friday

Acts 3:1–10

*One day Peter and John were going up to the temple
at the hour of prayer, at three o'clock in the afternoon.
And a man lame from birth was being carried in. People
would lay him daily at the gate of the temple called the
Beautiful Gate so that he could ask for alms from those
entering the temple.*

Acts 3:1–2

The Beautiful Gate

The man, lame from birth the Scripture tells us, gets
carried to the Beautiful Gate, on the cusp of the temple. Every day this person asks for alms from the faithful
on their way to worship. Every day others carry him to
this spot where he attempts to get by on the charity of
God's people as they go to hear the law and the prophets,
words about loving neighbor and caring for the vulnerable. Given that this man must be taken to the Beautiful
Gate daily, his efforts clearly do not provide him with any

sustainable security. Then as now, a safety net for those unable to provide fully for themselves was lacking.

On this day, Peter and John are going to pray at the temple and rather than look away or walk past quickly, as so often we do when we see a need we assume we cannot meet, they "direct their gaze at him." Peter instructs the man: "Look at us." The man complies, expecting to receive some money, but instead Peter and John offer him the wholeness that comes with Jesus Christ. This miracle story is one of restoration to community, as miracle stories often are. The man, barred due to his infirmity from the temple, now enters with others to praise God. He enters the temple with them. Instead of a cursory glance, the disciples regard the man on the edge of society. Instead of a spare coin, the disciples share the abundant life they received through the Messiah. They see him and, through the power of the Holy Spirit, join their fate with his as they praise God together.

When we read these biblical stories of Jesus' followers healing and even raising the dead, we may well think, that was then and this is now, such miracles do not happen anymore. And yet, Jesus tells us that we will accomplish even more than he did. We do not need to settle for the status quo of the hurting being relegated to sit beside the beautiful gate but never enter into the fullness of life proclaimed just on the other side of it. Disciples of Jesus Christ look directly at suffering and trust that God wills to relieve it, through us. Bringing those on the margins fully into community begins with seeing each person as beloved and worthy of regard. Peter and John offer what they have: the love of God poured out, the compassion of Christ made known in tangible acts of justice, the fellowship of the Holy Spirit evident in radical hospitality and courageous kindness.

Like Peter and John, we refuse to step around the injured, ignore the isolated, or exploit the vulnerable. We who follow the Savior who came into the world as a helpless infant seek to see beauty not only in grand and sacred architecture, but in flawed and finite people, knowing the Messiah came to heal the sick, proclaim good news to the poor, and to save sinners.

Questions for Reflection

1. This week, notice who you encounter on the way to worship. Who is at the beautiful gates, the edges of our communities? What would it mean to see them? What do you have to give them?
2. Have you ever experienced being unable to bring anything less than your best self to worship? Why do we think that we have to have it all together to come to church?
3. Who are you in this story? Peter or John? The man lame from birth? The people who carry the man to the Beautiful Gate? Imagine yourself in this scene: How do you sense God's presence and power?

Prayer for the Day

Lord of power and might, you sent your Son to heal and teach, preach and save, forgive and show mercy. Jesus saw those on the edges of society. He stopped for those who called to him for help. He welcomed the children and touched those deemed untouchable. Do not let those of us who claim his name neglect our siblings sitting at the very gates of our churches. Give us the faith to proclaim the love of Christ and offer the right hand of fellowship so that we can enter your temple together in worship and in praise. May the beauty of our actions outshine even the most glorious of our sanctuaries. Amen.

Saturday

Acts 21:27–36

The whole city was aroused, and the people came running from all directions. Seizing Paul, they dragged him from the temple, and immediately the gates were shut.

Acts 21:30 NIV

Shut Gates

Chaos erupts due to Paul's preaching. Rioting ensues due to Paul's proclamation and, it should not be lost, because he brings Gentiles into the temple. Which of these actions, I wonder, causes more of an uproar? The message or the crossing of cultural, religious, tribal boundaries? Few happenings elicit more ire than threatening people's perceived turf, power, and control. Paul's sermon of a Savior of the world, embodied by the joining of radically different peoples, gets him thrown out of the temple, gates shut behind him, beaten and arrested. God may well be the Lord of all that is, seen and unseen, but human beings like our categories, our customs, and our divisions.

Why? What is at stake for us in keeping our communities homogeneous? What appeals to us about border walls and locked gates that keep some out and others safely inside? While visiting Scotland, I learned of their "freedom to roam" laws. So long as one respects others' land and closes gates behind them, one is allowed to wander over land and have access to inland water. I learned of this act by way of a tour guide who had visited the United States and been told not to explore as if he were in Scotland, mind the fences, gates, and "No Trespassing" signs. Shut gates and property lines matter in the U.S. and crossing them could get you arrested, or worse.

Why? What do we fear? What do we want to keep to ourselves? Who do we want to keep at bay? This tumultuous story from the book of Acts calls us to examine our propensity to not simply reject God's barrier-busting Word, but attack those who speak it and do everything in our power to silence both the message and the messenger. We attempt to shut all manner of gates to the life-saving power of the gospel. The gospel says forgive as you have been forgiven, and yet we shut that gate tightly and seek vengeance. The gospel says care for the least of these, and yet we go into our safe havens and shut the gates behind us, leaving Lazarus begging on the curb. The gospel says welcome the stranger, and yet we demand a wall be built, gates locked and guarded, to keep the asylum seeker out of "our" country. The gospel says we are one through Christ Jesus our Lord, and yet for years white Christians shut the gates of their hearts and minds, justifying slavery through the very Scripture that said that there is no Jew nor Greek, slave nor free, male nor female.

The world-claiming, people-joining, reconciling, embodied Word stirs up the crowd, reorders the status quo, and more often than not causes those in positions of privilege to shut their gates and seek to silence those who speak and enact God's transformative gospel. As we make ready for the coming of the One whose birth is good news of great joy for all people, are we prepared to be joined with everyone whom Jesus comes to save?

Questions for Reflection

1. When have you been offended by the expansiveness of the gospel? Of God's love? Grace? Forgiveness?
2. Have you ever been excluded from a place where you'd hoped to be welcomed? Been locked out of a shut gate, either literally or metaphorically? How did that feel?
3. Read the Acts passage again; what is so offensive about it that it causes people to violently attack Paul?

Prayer for the Day

Jesus, Savior of the world, we find your expansive grace offensive. While we yearn for your mercy for ourselves, we resent forgiveness extended to others. You come to save sinners and we are solidly in that category, but we imagine our failings not as grievous as those of other people. We conveniently forget that the earth and all that is within it belong to you and instead claim creation for ourselves, even when you call on us to let go of everything and follow you, to lose our very lives for your sake. Send your Spirit and open any of the gates we have shut to your life-giving Word. Amen.

Second Week of Advent

Tears

Sunday

Psalm 80

O LORD God of hosts,
  how long will you be angry with your people's prayers?
You have fed them with the bread of tears,
  and given them tears to drink in full measure.

Psalm 80:4–5

Bread of Tears

A diet of tears, salty tears that only heighten thirst, days of aching, seasons of longing, times when prayers feel more like groans than discernible words—everyone serves terms of intense suffering. How long, O Lord God, will you be angry with our prayers and seemingly refuse to hear and answer? Lament springs from the depths of our individual or collective pain and we call out to a God we doubt listens or even exists, and yet cry out we do.

How long, O Lord God, will you let our loved one languish with dementia? How long, O Lord God, will my beloved reside in the valley of depression? How long, O Lord, will my difficulty paying the bills last? How long, O Lord God of hosts, must the public health crisis threaten our safety and health and economy? How long, O Lord God, will inequity persist and the arc of history resist the bend of justice? How long must we attempt to sustain ourselves on a diet of tears?

As twinkling lights populate yards and jaunty holiday music plays in every store and the secular message is one of sentimental happiness, the psalmist's talk of eating and drinking tears feels inappropriate or even disrespectful and rude. However, the message of Advent is not one of superficial optimism, but rather one of tenacious hope. Jesus becomes incarnate not because the world overflows with peace, joy, kindness, patience, and justice. Jesus comes to earth in order to bring light to those who sit in deep darkness.

The birth of Jesus, the colliding of the mystery of divinity with the finitude of humanity, means that nothing, no feeling, no experience, no question, no doubt, no pain, are off-limits to God's redemptive power and saving grace. Jesus himself knows the diet of tear-filled bread and water, his mother, Mary, does too. Do not be ashamed of screaming, "O Lord God of hosts, how long will you be angry with your people's prayers?" That groan from the dark night of the soul reverberates through history and all the way up to heaven. That cry is answered by Immanuel, God with us, no matter what.

Flannery O'Connor, in the book of her essays, *Mysteries and Manners*, writes this about grace: "It is . . . simply a concern with the human reaction to that which, instant by instant, gives life to the soul. It is a concern with a realization that breeds charity and with the charity that breeds action. Often the nature of grace can be made plain only by describing its absence."*

As we anticipate Christ's coming, we may well need to tend, instant by instant, to that which gives even fleeting life to our souls and to the souls of others. Our desperate prayers, our bread of tears, may be that which keeps us alive until we experience Immanuel. Our descriptions of grace's absence, even as our culture sings "Jingle Bells" and tells us that we can buy our way to fulfillment, may well be the stories that reveal plainly the light no darkness can overcome.

Questions for Reflection:

1. When have you cried with the psalmist: How long, O Lord God of hosts? How did your lament help sustain you until you felt relief?
2. What is the bread of tears you have had to eat? What about those in your neighborhood? Our country? World? How can that bread of tears be replaced with the bread of life?
3. Do you ever feel as if the weeks before Christmas in our culture make it difficult to express feelings of lament and sadness? How do we make room for those who may find this season not one of delight but one of pain?

Prayer for the Day

How long, O Lord God of hosts, will you be angry with your people's prayers? How long will you seem to refuse to hear our cries for relief? How long will you stay far from us, Lord God?

---

*Flannery O'Connor, *Mystery and Manners: Occasional Prose*, ed. Sally and Robert Fitzgerald (New York: Farrar, Straus & Giroux, 1969), 204.

Trusting no feeling or experience is off-limits to your redemptive grace, Lord of hosts, we cry out to you in our weakness and sorrow without shame or embarrassment. We pour out our hearts to the One who sends Immanuel to save us. We wait for your face to shine upon us, the light no darkness can overcome. We wait in hope even as we pray in anguish. Amen.

Monday

Jeremiah 13:15–17

But if you will not listen,
my soul will weep in secret for your pride;
my eyes will weep bitterly and run down with tears,
because the LORD's flock has been taken captive.
Jeremiah 13:17

Bitter Tears

The prophet Jeremiah listens to God and proclaims what the Lord tells him to say to God's people. Jeremiah, that weeping prophet, must speak hard truths to a beloved people who refuse to hear and heed the word of the Lord. Calling out the sins and failings of one's own tribe rarely, if ever, engenders respect or affection from one's siblings. Nonetheless, Jeremiah attempts to instruct the people to listen to the Lord their God or else endure the consequences of their refusal to be who God created and called them to be. Bitter tears come as a result of seeing those one loves act in self-destructive ways. Bitter tears flow when one cannot prevent those one loves from hurting themselves and others.

No wonder Jeremiah weeps bitter and copious tears. What could be worse than watching a preventable disaster of their own making befall one's own people? What could be more difficult than being chosen to be the prophet to speak these harsh words to those for whom one cares deeply? And yet, Jeremiah can do no other; even when he wants to refuse this heavy call, he cannot. He laments, "If I say, 'I will not mention him, or speak any more in his name,' then within me there is something like a burning fire shut up in my bones; I am weary with holding it in, and I cannot" (Jer. 20:9). Despite his bitter tears, Jeremiah is overpowered by God's call and cannot keep God's word to himself. He may well be the laughing stock of his own people, and yet God's call to keep the covenant refuses to go unspoken.

Cathleen Kaveny reminds us of the point of harsh verses of judgment such as these in her book *Prophecy without Contempt: Religious Discord in the Public Square*. She writes,

> The purpose of prophetic indictments is to call attention, in the sharpest possible terms, to fundamental moral flaws in a given society or culture, flaws that threaten to undermine the basic tenets of the moral vision animating that society. Accordingly, the sharp language of prophetic speech is designed to pierce through layers of apathy and motivate the audience to repent, reform and ameliorate the underlying situation.*

*Cathleen Kaveny, *Prophecy without Contempt: Religious Discourse in the Public Square* (Cambridge, MA: Harvard University Press, 2016), 331.

Some situations warrant bitter and prolonged tears. Sometimes a culture's behavior is so egregious and counter to God's will that only stark words of judgment and a naming of inevitable consequences will do.

As we journey toward Bethlehem, we must remember that Advent also calls us to remember that the Risen Christ will return, and when he does he will separate the sheep and the goats based on how our culture treated the least of these. Jeremiah's bitter tears, painful as the impending exile that prompts them is, are ignored at our peril. While we do not like to think about God's judgment, we must if we are to cut through layers of apathy, repent and repair those circumstances in our time that cause not only the prophet to cry bitter tears, but Jesus to weep too.

Questions for Reflection

1. When have you tried to prevent someone you love from engaging in self-destructive behavior? When has someone who loves you attempted to speak a hard truth to you? What happened?
2. If the prophetic indictment is designed to provoke repentance and change, what is the prophet condemning in our time that is counter to the will of God?
3. When have you wept bitter tears?

Prayer for the Day

Lord who weeps with those who weep, we come to you chastened and ready to repent and be changed. We place ourselves in your mercy as we seek to listen to and be transformed by your judgment. Do not let us turn away from your tears. When we neglect your commandments, send prophets to speak hard truths to us out of love. When we forget your call to us to proclaim your word in season and out of season, make your message burn in our bones until we open our mouths and speak boldly your life-giving, transformative gospel until Christ comes again, and come again he will. Amen.

Tuesday

Ecclesiastes 4:1–12

Again I saw all the oppressions that are practiced under the sun. Look, the tears of the oppressed—with no one to comfort them! On the side of their oppressors there was power—with no one to comfort them.

Ecclesiastes 4:1

Tears of the Oppressed

The tears of the oppressed run through the streets. Despair grows with justice denied. Unrest rises with inequities left intact for centuries. The tears of the oppressed represent not just sorrow and suffering, but righteous anger that will not be silenced forever. The global pandemic of 2020 brought with it waves of tears, tears of mourning for the dead buried without the full rituals of funerals, tears of anxiety when layoffs reverberated across the land, tears of fear for those without access to health care. Then, two months into the health crisis, came the murder of George Floyd and the heaving of a nation that followed. The oppressed wept publicly and no longer could the source of their pain be denied.

Jesus' earthly ministry begins with a visit to his home faith community and his subsequent rejection by his own people. He stands in the synagogue on that sabbath and reads from the prophet Isaiah, "'The Spirit of the Lord is upon me, because he has anointed me to bring good news to the poor. He has sent me to proclaim release to the captives and recovery of sight to the blind, to let the oppressed go free, to proclaim the year of the Lord's favor'" (Luke 4:18–19). And all who knew him best are filled with pride and affirmation until he interprets the text and tells his own people that they may in fact not be the ones for whom this is good news. He calls them out, calls them to account, compels them to look at themselves and ask if they are indeed the ones in need of release or the ones holding others captive. Needless to say, the congregation responds with indignation, anger, running him out and pushing him to the brink of a cliff. Not exactly a resoundingly successful start to the Savior's ministry.

This Jesus on whom we wait this Advent season brings good news of great joy for all people and this means that the tears of the oppressed will not go unseen, unheard, uncomforted. The One who comes to proclaim release to the captives will no doubt anger the people who benefit from the captivity. Good news for the poor entails a redistribution of wealth and power, and this kind of justice does not come without great resistance. The question those of us anticipating Immanuel must ask ourselves is this: Are we willing to participate in the good news of great joy for all people, even if it costs us something? If we are those in power, will we for the sake of our Lord join our cries with those of the oppressed and work for the justice that rolls like a roaring water, washing away the tears of our siblings too long left without comfort? We must not forget that the infant for whom we wait is the Messiah who brings good news to the poor, the ascended Lord who judges between those who cared for the least of these, or not, and the returning Risen Christ who comforts the oppressed.

Questions for Reflection

1. Read the headlines today: Where are the oppressed crying and how are they being comforted, or not?
2. How is Jesus' coming good news for all people? How does this good news for all people impact the choices you make? How you treat others?
3. What is our Christian responsibility to responding to the tears of the oppressed?

Prayer for the Day

Lord, we see your children, our siblings, crying in the streets for justice. The tears of the oppressed water the way of those too long denied comfort, equity, and abundant life. Our Savior comes to release the captives and bring relief to those who suffer. As we make ready for his birth, may our preparations be sacrificial, not superficial. May we weep with those who weep and work for a way of life together that reflects your good news of great joy for all people. Do not let us be among those who reject Jesus because our desire for power outweighs our love of you and our neighbors. Amen.

Wednesday

Psalm 126

May those who sow in tears
reap with shouts of joy.
Those who go out weeping,
bearing the seed for sowing,
shall come home with shouts of joy,
carrying their sheaves.
Psalm 126:5–6

Sown Tears

This psalm is one of hard-won praise, not a sentimental or superficial good feeling, but words of gratitude to God that spring from places of deep pain and sorrow. In Amor Towles' novel *A Gentleman in Moscow*, Count Rostov, under house arrest at a luxury hotel in the years after the Russian Revolution, talks about being a member of the confederacy of the humbled. The count, a waiter in the very place he once was served, notes,

[H]aving fallen suddenly from grace, those in the Confederacy share a certain perspective. Knowing beauty, influence, fame, and privilege to be borrowed rather than bestowed, they are not easily impressed. They are not quick to envy or take offense. They certainly do not scour the papers in search of their own names. They remain committed to living among their peers, but they greet adulation with caution, ambition with sympathy, and condescension with an inward smile.*

Their praise grows rich with knowing what it means to live in the shadow of the valley of death for unknown lengths of time. Their tears have sown their shouts of joy. Their sense of themselves and the world reflects a perspective tempered with the truth of our human finitude and fragility.

Jesus seems to seek out those who know what it means to sow long seasons of tears. He goes to the demoniac tethered to the grave, the lepers excommunicated from society, the woman chronically ill for eighteen years, the tax collectors despised by their own people, the woman about to be stoned for adultery. Those humbled by circumstances, some out of their control and some of their own making, provide soil fertilized by tears and subsequently ripe for receiving the seeds of the gospel that brings forth shouts of relieved, resurrected joy.

In a church I served early in my ministry, I came to count on the wisdom of a leader in the church whose counsel and presence never failed to encourage. She laughed easily, worked tirelessly to help the vulnerable,

---

*Amor Towles, *A Gentleman in Moscow* (New York: Viking, 2016), 196.

and exhibited a compassion to everyone that I can only aspire to emulate. When I needed not just an instructive word but one of hopeful faith, I called her. I learned that when she was a young mother she had been diagnosed with an aggressive form of cancer, not given good odds for survival, and told to prepare for brutal treatment that may or may not save her life. She endured rounds of chemotherapy, multiple surgeries, radiation, and all the pain that accompanied it, all while attempting to tend to her preschool-age children. When I came to know her, those children were grown and having children of their own. Miraculously, she survived and remained cancer-free. Her tears had sown in her a great joy for life and given her a humility and gentleness through which she saw the world as a result. Having gotten to the other side of a near-death experience, she praised God for every moment, no matter how mundane. I loved working with her because her answer to whatever was before us, whatever request, whatever challenge, was an unwavering sense that with God's help, we would figure it out. Her tears had sown an abundant harvest of hard-won faith that she in turn shared joyously with the world.

Questions for Reflection
1. When have you sown in tears and reaped in joy?
2. Do you know people who are members of "the confederacy of the humbled"? What do you notice about them? Are you a member of that group?
3. How do we encourage those still sowing in tears, yet to reap in joy?

Prayer for the Day
God, hear the cries of those sowing fields of tears this day, the sick, the lonely, the fearful. Do not let their weeping be in vain.

Do not let it last forever. When we crumble under the weight of our sorrow, unsure if we will ever shout for joy again, send the Comforter, your Holy Spirit, to encourage and sustain us. When you bring us home from exile, whatever form that season of pain takes, may our shouts of joy resound through our communities, bearing witness to your goodness, grace, and mercy, granting hope to those still sowing in tears. Amen.

Thursday

Luke 7:36–49

She stood behind him at his feet, weeping, and began to bathe his feet with her tears and to dry them with her hair. Then she continued kissing his feet and anointing them with the ointment.

Luke 7:38

Uncontrollable Tears

What possessed her to seek out Jesus, at a well-known Pharisee's home no less, and make a public spectacle of herself? The writer of Luke's Gospel reveals only that she is a sinner. The Pharisee, repulsed by this display, scandalized by her impropriety, thinks Jesus ought to know what kind of woman she is and put an end to her disruption of their nice dinner party. I resonate all too well with the Pharisee's discomfort at this woman's unchecked emotional outburst. I get uncomfortable just reading this story. I do not so much want to send the woman away as take her aside and whisper, "This is not the time nor the place. Perhaps you could talk to Jesus, privately, later." I cringe at her lack of control and unselfconsciousness.

What's that phrase? Never let them see you sweat? Or, fake it until you make it? How about, keep calm and carry on? Explicitly and implicitly, I learned not to let my feelings show. To do so reveals weakness, vulnerability. In a work setting, tears were verboten. Unprofessional. In middle school, when I was the subject of several years of teasing, my parents' advice entailed steeling myself so as not to reveal that my peers were "getting" to me. Practice that ridiculous idiom about sticks and stones and words not hurting. Suck it up, button up, buck up, soldier on. Do not make a scene. As quickly and politely as possible, escort this distraught woman out of the building. Except . . . she refuses to cooperate. She cannot contain her love for Jesus, her relief at the possibility of being seen as something other than the label "sinner," her tears of repentance that open the way to rebirth.

Nothing, no one, can prevent this woman's total, embodied response to the person and grace of the incarnate Messiah. And Jesus tells the Pharisee, and all of us appalled at her person and her behavior, that her tears and her touch, her weeping and her outpouring of precious ointment, is absolutely appropriate, right and good. Her uncontrollable, over-the-top reaction to Jesus ought to be ours too.

A wise woman I knew years ago, a retired teacher committed to ministries of compassion, composed and confident, told me a story one evening after a long, contentious church meeting in which I allowed my frustration to show. She saw my hurt at the outcome of the discussion around a ministry close to my heart. I expressed my disappointment to her not so much at the results of the meeting as at my inability to keep my emotions about them in check and hidden. She said as a new teacher she once broke down and cried in her classroom when a student said something hurtful to her. She felt embarrassed and weak. The next day, however, the student apologized. She said her tears surprised the student and her vulnerability, unwanted though it was, enabled them to have a genuine relationship. She told me that my response in that meeting perhaps revealed the importance of the issue before us. Some things, she said, are worth crying about, and how will others know their importance if we refuse to be moved by them?

Questions for Reflection

1. Have you ever been overcome with emotions, even when you wanted to control them? What moved you? How did others respond to you?
2. When have you been called upon to be present to someone inconsolable? How did you handle their vulnerability?
3. When have you come to Jesus and poured yourself out to him? How did Jesus respond to you?

Prayer of the Day

Lord, you do not send us away when we come to you in tears, overwhelmed by our need for your mercy. When we hold back our tears and keep our emotions in check in order to save face or appear to be in control, you urge us to be honest about our sin, our failings, and our total reliance on your grace. You honor our vulnerability and meet it with compassion and forgiveness. When we kneel at your feet and pour ourselves out, you look at us with love and set us free to live in right relationship with you and others. Amen.

Friday

2 Timothy 1:1–7

Recalling your tears, I long to see you so that I may be filled with joy.

2 Timothy 1:4

Remembered Tears

Longing marks this season. Nostalgia creeps around the corner and then all but wrestles me to the ground as I unwrap Christmas ornaments from years past and place them on the tree. My firstborn's first grade handprint crafted into Santa, the snowman with the name of a child in need that my husband and I bought gifts for our first year of marriage, the "baby's first Christmas" Lenox rocking horse, shells decoupaged with winter scenes made by my mother-in-law when her son was little. Each one calls forth visions of people, places, and experiences that stretched and shaped me. I cannot rush through the process because to do so seems disrespectful. These quirky items feel akin to holy relics.

How many trees have donned these priceless treasures? Will they be passed down to my children years from now? If so, what memories will they evoke? Will they think of the many evenings we lit candles on the Advent wreath? The Christmas morning the new puppy escaped out the front door? Our holiday tradition of eating at Waffle House? I pray their recollections bring forth mostly happiness and a keen sense of being loved, even when their parents made mistakes.

Paul longs to see his mentee and friend, Timothy, wishes desperately he could see him face-to-face. When I hold that glass angel with the gold trim in my hand, the one given to me by my grandfather no telling how many years ago, I long to see him again too. I cannot help but get wistful recalling the delight of my children when they woke up at dawn eager to unpack their stockings and unwrap their gifts. Recalling comes hand in hand with expecting during Advent.

While I prepare for Jesus' birth and Christ's coming, looking ahead to the promised new thing that God is surely doing, I cannot help but look back, often with tears, tears of joy and tears of loss. The decorations and music, the cards and church services overflow with memories and meaning. I am no longer cajoling a toddler to wear an itchy shepherd's costume for the live nativity or putting together complicated toys at midnight. The stress of those days still comes to consciousness, but recalling even the difficult aspects of those days brings tears, mostly tears of gratitude. Tears of longing, too. I miss those I will not see face-to-face this year. Nonetheless, I do not long so much to go back, but rather long to make sure I look forward in hope, with thanksgiving, anticipating God present and coming. I yearn to make sure I appreciate the gift of this

Advent with all its challenges and blessings. Recalling all those of past years reminds me to relish this one.

I am reminded of all the saints who shaped my life and my faith, my grandparents and parents, children and friends, all of whom envelop me in a spirit of love that brings with it tears of joy.

Questions for Reflection

1. What do you recall this year that brings tears to your eyes?
2. Who taught you the faith? Shaped it? Remember them and give thanks for them.
3. For what or whom are you longing this year?

Prayer for the Day

Lord of our past, present, and future, this season brings with it powerful and poignant memories. We recall people and places that have shaped us and tested us. We remember times of joy and times of sorrow. We cannot help but look back even as we anticipate and prepare for your birth and victorious return. We know that you are present and at work in all seasons. Our tears do not go unnoticed to you. Your Spirit gives us the power of love that sustains us in all things and at all times. Amen.

Saturday

Revelation 7:9–17

"They will hunger no more, and thirst no more;
the sun will not strike them,
nor any scorching heat;
for the Lamb at the center of the throne will be their
shepherd,
and he will guide them to springs of the water of life,
and God will wipe away every tear from their eyes."

Revelation 7:16–17

Wiped Tears

We know how the story ends. Brian Blount, a New Testament scholar and president of Union Presbyterian Seminary, talks about the power of knowing how the story turns out, knowing that ultimately God's justice and love prevails. This knowledge gives us the courage for the living of these days. No matter the challenges and travails, we followers of Jesus Christ persist in doing justice, loving kindness and walking humbly with the God whose home is among mortals, the God who becomes mortal, the God who will wipe every tear from the eyes of those who have known great suffering. The description of heavenly worship in Revelation 7 paints a picture that inspires us to strive for God's kingdom, so near and yet so far away on earth.

Every tribe and nation, together praising God around the throne of grace. Would that this were so right now in our congregations. Every tribe and every nation kept safe and secure under the shelter of the One on that throne. Would that we made that vision a reality in the here and now and not just a hope for the sweet bye and bye. All peoples, all languages, the richness and beauty of their cultures not erased or consumed, but gloriously intact as they worship the one God and creator of us all. What if we began each day reading these words, envisioning this holy promise, bringing God's future into our present in ways big and small?

In his book *The Invasion of the Dead: Preaching Resurrection*, Blount admonishes preachers "to preach God's future life in the midst of a dead now."* He writes,

> In terms of social justice, economic equality, environmental care, international politics, you name it, the questions arise: Do we see what such an issue looks like from the perspective of God's future? And if we do see such a future, what are we prepared in the present to preach about it?†

I would widen Blount's call to include not just preachers and preaching but also Christians and living. If we see

---

*Brian Blount, *Invasion of the Dead: Preaching Resurrection* (Louisville, KY: Westminster John Knox Press, 2014), 77.

†Blount, *Invasion of the Dead*, 104.

every tear as one that God will wipe dry in the future, are we prepared to ameliorate the circumstances that elicit that weeping right here and now, for Christ's sake?

If we who prepare for Jesus' birth and anticipate Christ's return know the end of the story, God's promise to wipe every tear, alleviate hunger and thirst, gather together people from north, south, east and west, what are we prepared to do, in Blount's words, to "raise our vision up and forward,"* make manifest the prayer we pray week in and week out, that God's will be done, on earth as it is in heaven?

As we journey through Advent bombarded by worldly headlines of division, violence, upheaval, and suffering, can we remember that Jesus is coming not to condemn the world, as condemnation-worthy as it often seems, but instead to save it? Can we remember that the Messiah comes that we might have life and life abundant, and participate in this life-giving God-vision? Knowing that God will wipe every tear from every eye, will we get a head start on that intimate, loving, unquestionably present comfort now? If we know God's promised future, can we who follow the Incarnate Lord help embody it in the present, no matter the cost or risk such counterculture living requires?

Questions for Reflection

1. When you read these verses from Revelation, what emotions do they evoke in you?
2. Have you ever had an experience that gave you a glimpse on earth of this heavenly worship?
3. When have you had your tears wiped dry by another? When have you helped console someone else?

*Blount, *Invasion of the Dead*, 103.

Prayer for the Day

To the One on the throne, we worship you. Lost in wonder and praise, we gather to give thanks for your steadfast love, your providential care, your commitment to making your home among us. When our tears flow in the face of earthly suffering, we remember your promised future when crying will be no more and all will be safe, together, valued and whole. May that sure ending compel us in faith to bring your future into our present. May your will be done on earth, as it is in heaven. Amen.

Third Week of Advent

Belts

Sunday

Isaiah 11:1–9

Righteousness shall be the belt around his waist,
and faithfulness the belt around his loins.
Isaiah 11:5

Belt of Righteousness

The Savior soon-to-become incarnate ushers in a peaceable kingdom difficult for us to imagine possible. The One sent by God reverses what seems like an intractable order of the strong suppressing the weak, of those on the top of the social order getting more and more resources at the expense of those below them, of endless wars and perpetual exploitation of creation. Isaiah's vision soars as the prophet sets forth a holy agenda ripe with all we thought impossible: equity will be enacted for the meek, the wolf and the lamb will lie down together, the earth will be full of the knowledge of the Lord. The headlines of our age and every age before us will be replaced with a counter narrative of the oppressed receiving justice, violence not only ending but reconciliation and lasting peace the order of the day. Imagine. Can we?

Part of the challenge of glorious texts like this one from Isaiah is our inability to accept that these words are prescriptive, descriptive, not simply lovely poetry to assuage our weary souls. In an age ripe with cynicism and skepticism, reading about divine wisdom and understanding, delight and faithfulness feels quaint, maybe even indulgent. Do we not need to face the facts? Get real and get to work? We do strategic plans and analyze the data and prepare the budgets and set our achievable goals, not just in our secular workplaces, but in our faith communities too. Cost benefit, risk management, return on investment, all of these concepts dictate our choices and often truncate our imagination.

The Savior for whom we wait and prepare is wrapped in a belt of righteousness, he is clothed in faithfulness. He traffics in miracles, not data, relationships, not transactions. His ministry upends the calculus of efficiency and biggest bang for one's buck. He leaves the ninety-nine sheep and goes to find the one. He takes time to welcome little children and makes enemies of the most powerful. He eats with tax collectors, touches those deemed untouchable, and allows society's outcasts to touch him. He spends the most time with people incapable of connecting him to a network of wealthy supporters or protective patrons. This belt of righteousness upholds justice for the poor and extends care for the weak. God's wraparound righteousness defies our earthly inclinations of enmity and fear of each other. Isaiah's vision, if we understand it to be performative language, expands our imagination and invites us to wrap ourselves with God's belt of righteousness and gird our loins with a faithfulness prepared to participate in holy possibilities. Imagine.

Masha Gessen writes in an article entitled, "The Threat of Moral Authority," about the need to reach for the "higher note." Gessen writes, "That higher note is a necessary condition of vision." That vision, in turn, is necessary in shaping a moral society. Gessen goes on to say, "Raw power can overtake moral authority, and perhaps today it is easier than ever before, but a determined effort to preserve ideals when they are under attack can serve as a bridge to the future."* This Advent, our Christian call entails putting on the belt of righteousness and preserving the ideals of delight, faithfulness, fear, and knowledge of the Lord, a peaceable kingdom. Imagine that certain, divine future.

Questions for Reflection

1. Read the passage from Isaiah slowly and imagine the picture it paints. Do you see glimpses of this vision in your life? In the world?
2. What would it mean for you to think about wearing a belt of righteousness? Of being wrapped with faithfulness?
3. What is the role of vision in shaping change both personally and as a community and culture?

Prayer for the Day

Loving God, as we anticipate the coming of the Christ child, we lament how limited our vision is. We give in to the prevailing sentiment that things never really change, that transformation is impossible, that self-protection should be our priority. Yet we hear the prophet's words of equity and justice, delight

---

*Masha Gessen, "The Threat of Moral Authority." *The New York Review*, 2017, https://www.nybooks.com/daily/2017/01/18/threat-of-moral -authority-john-lewis-trump/.

and wisdom, and our hope is kindled, our imagination stirred. Wrap us in your righteousness and clothe us in your faithfulness that we might see the world through the eyes of divine possibility and act out of holy inspiration. May we participate in the peaceable kingdom Jesus comes to bring. Amen.

Monday

Job 12:13–25

God pours contempt on princes,
and looses the belt of the strong.
God uncovers the deeps out of darkness,
and brings deep darkness to light.
Job 12:21–22

Loosened Belt

Job, a self-described laughingstock, responds to those well-intentioned friends who want to explain his own situation to him. Job knows better than anyone his faith and his loss, his grief and his dismay. Is there anything less helpful than others attempting to tell us how we feel, how we ought to react to painful circumstances, where God's providence lies in the midst of some of life's most challenging seasons? Many of us, no doubt searching for words of comfort, utter platitudes that engender more hurt rather than help. We trot out a verse of the Bible like "all things work together for good for those who love God" (Rom. 8:28). Perhaps we have been on the receiving end of a friend telling us in our mourning that "God needed another angel in heaven."

Such sentiments may well bring relief when we claim them as our own, but when other people impress them upon us, guilt over a lack of faith mixes with sorrow and hurt and we, like Job, may well feel like the laughingstock of our community, or worse, abandoned by the God we love. The words of this chapter of Job's story are Job's. Somehow, in the midst of his suffering, Job still manages to recognize God's expansive power. Maybe because of his suffering Job sees God's unmistakable control. Is it not when we are at our lowest that we confess our finitude and our utter hope in and need for God's power?

Job lists all of the creatures dependent upon God's provision, all of nature beholden to God's might, and then all the human beings of high status that God can bring down in an instant—counselors, judges, kings, priests, and princes. These people held in high esteem on earth cannot even claim mastery over their own clothing. God will loosen the belts of princes and they will go where God leads. Water, light, fish, birds, rulers, and, yes, Job, all are dependent upon the provisions, providence, and grace of God. The question for Job and for us when we are in great pain is whether this offers us hope or if it furthers our hurt. Is God's presence in our suffering one that provides comfort, or does it cause us to wonder why God does not intervene?

Christena Cleveland, in her article "So Much of the Privileged Life Is about Transcendence," poses this question, "What if we can't truly experience the hope of the Divine until we are able to experience the Divine in the most hopeless of situations?" She goes on to write, "Throughout human history, the oppressed peoples of the world have, out of necessity, intentionally turned their focus on

God in the midst of the most painful experiences."* Job, in recognizing God's greatness not despite his horrendous circumstances, but in the middle of them, comes to this hard-won knowledge, a knowledge that once experienced, never leaves, and alters one's perspective of self, God, and others forever. When we come to the revelation that God's mercy, love, and goodness persist even when our belts are loosened, our power gone, and we are utterly unable to alter our own reality, we rest solely in the promise of God's presence and promise to never abandon us. Then we know what it means to be free.

Questions for Reflection

1. When have you experienced wanting to comfort someone but not knowing how? What did you do or say?
2. When have you been in a painful place? Who helped you while you were hurting? What helped and what did not? Why?
3. Have you, like Job, come to a place of hard-won spiritual knowledge that God is present in suffering?

Prayer for the Day

Lord, your mercies are new every morning, but some seasons we find it hard to recognize your grace. Knowing you are our creator, redeemer, and sustainer, we look to you for hope, comfort, and strength. Give us the faith to know your presence and trust your providential care even during unspeakably hard times. When we sit with others who suffer, do not let us silence their cries when their pain makes us uncomfortable. Send your Spirit to strengthen our resolve to remain in those hard places until we are able to see the dawn break through the dark. Amen.

---

*Christena Cleveland, "So Much of the Privileged Life Is about Transcendence," *On Being*, July 07, 2017, https://onbeing.org/blog/christena–cleveland–so–much–of–the–privileged–life–is–about–transcendence/.

Tuesday

Jeremiah 13:1–11

For as the loincloth clings to one's loins, so I made the whole
house of Israel and the whole house of Judah cling to me,
says the LORD, in order that they might be for me a people,
a name, a praise, and a glory. But they would not listen.
Jeremiah 13:11

Useless Belt

"Loincloth" might also be translated as "waistcloth" or
"girdle" or "belt." In other words, that piece of clothing
that is closest to our bodies, hidden to almost everyone
else, but unmistakably present to us as we go about our
day. God in this passage gives Jeremiah detailed instructions on conducting an experiment with a waistcloth, that
intimate item of clothing worn underneath other garments. In this exchange God tells Jeremiah to remove
this belt of cloth, the very one he is wearing, and hide it
in the cleft of a rock, leaving it for many days, until that
time God tells him to retrieve it. Jeremiah does as he is
told and discovers the belt rotted and "good for nothing."

Then God makes God's point: that once protective and close item of clothing, cast aside and buried, becomes utterly useless, just like my people who refuse such intimacy with me.

God wanted a close relationship with Israel and Judah. God wanted to be as close to them as the belt around their waists, a daily presence that goes with them everywhere, but the people refused the gift of that close communion with the divine and instead tossed God aside, leaving their relationship to decompose and disintegrate. They forgot who and whose they were and subsequently they lost their purpose of praising and glorifying God. In short, they would not listen to the God who created, loved, and called them; when that relationship gets neglected, all others get misordered.

True intimacy does not come easily. Often, we reject the opportunity to know and be known honestly and fully. We want to hide behind layers of clothing that cover our flaws and present our best features to the world. We would rather not let others know our vulnerabilities lest they exploit or belittle them. We even attempt to keep parts of ourselves off-limits to God, refusing to listen to God's commandments and promises because we do not want to cede control and therefore enter into a relationship with God that requires us to open our hearts fully to all God loves. God wants to be as close as a belt wrapped around our waist, but we fear that nearness will be constricting rather than comforting. However, if we take off that inner garment, nothing else feels or fits right. Rejecting God prevents our other relationships from flourishing and reflecting holy priorities.

Our lives will reveal that which we hold dear, that which we love, that which we cling to closely. God says, "I made you to cling to me." Not material wealth. Not the affirmation of the world. Not your work. Not even your family and friends. Not your worries and fears. Not your outward appearance or inward insecurities. God offers us an intimacy that values us, cares for us, wants the best for us, gives us purpose, meaning and peace. Will we risk entering this intimate relationship or will we reject the One who shows us who we are made to be?

Questions for Reflection:
1. Is it strange to think of God as close to you as a belt, waistcloth, underwear? What is helpful or uncomfortable about this metaphor?
2. When have you clung to God? What did that clinging entail? Did you feel as if God was holding you in return?
3. How do we tend an intimate relationship with God? How does cultivating our relationship with God impact all of our other relationships?

Prayer for the Day
God of genuine intimacy and authentic relationship, you invite us to cling to you as we navigate even our most chaotic and frightening days. You offer to be as close to us as the cloth around our waist, present with us wherever we go. Forgive us when we reject you, your guidance, your call. Help us to recognize when we cast aside our relationship with you and exchange true intimacy for superficial worldly attachments. Send your Spirit to help us listen to your word so that our lives are rightly ordered and all our relationships are reflective of your will. Amen.

Wednesday

Matthew 3:1–6

Now John wore clothing of camel's hair with a leather belt around his waist, and his food was locusts and wild honey.
Matthew 3:4

Leather Belt

John the Baptist, Jesus' cousin, was a Nazarite. Set apart from his birth, the angel Gabriel announced that John would not drink strong drink and would be filled with the Holy Spirit. Matthew gives us a run down on John's clothing and diet, none of which sounds very appealing. Itchy, austere wardrobe, strange and limited diet, coupled with a message of repentance, certainly he stood out, but not, one would imagine, in a good way. And yet people flocked to him, were baptized by him, sought his advice. How is this possible? Would people do likewise today?

John's clothing recalled another holy person in the Bible, likely known to those coming to John when he emerged from the wilderness. John's camel hair cloak and leather belt brought to mind Elijah, that prophet who defeated Baal and ascended to heaven, the one, so the story goes, who would return prior to the Messiah's coming. Perhaps those in Jesus' day remembered this story and were attracted to his noteworthy appearance rather than repelled by it. No doubt, then as now, people were seeking meaning, direction, purpose, and an unmistakable sense of the divine. When John quoted the prophet Isaiah in his ancient garb, telling the masses that the kingdom of God was near, they wanted to believe it was true and hence they came to repent and be baptized.

Is it so different now? When the world feels turbulent (and frankly when has the world not felt more or less out of control?), people look for the assurance of meaning, hope, and the possibility for transformation. Hence, all the charlatans, religious and otherwise, who prey on people's fears and vulnerabilities, selling cures and prayers, offering God-given prosperity in exchange for a love offering, a sure reading of the future through the stars or cards. We yearn to know God's nearness and how our lives fit into the divine plan. Perhaps as off-putting as John appears, we, too, would have gone to him, confessed our sins, and been dunked in the water.

How, though, do we discern who is a messenger sent from God from who is only claiming the holy as a means of serving themselves? How they present themselves ought to be a clue. John's camel hair represents repentance, his leather belt unadorned and functional. His message runs counter to what those in power want to hear. John does not cozy up to power. John points away from himself and toward Jesus. He does not shy away from proclaiming a difficult word. Repentance requires real change, not a blessing of the status quo or a divine endorsement of those who could make John's life easy. John's outward appearance reveals an inward commitment to do God's will no matter the cost.

Do the people and places we flock to for divine guidance do likewise? If those who proclaim themselves to be about the work of the Lord serve themselves, sacrifice nothing, or seek only to please those with the power to make their own lives easier, then perhaps we ought to look elsewhere for God's word and will. Camel hair and leather belts, in and of themselves, do not guarantee a prophet's legitimacy, but if their words and deeds match their outward appearance, perhaps we ought to pay attention and assess if there is continuity between what we say we value and how we live. If not, John's invitation still holds: "Repent, for the kingdom of heaven has come near" (Matt. 3:2).

Questions for Reflection
1. When have you sought out direction or change in your life? From whom did you seek that direction? What happened?
2. How do you discern the difference between God's word and a random voice crying out in the wilderness?
3. In this Advent season, how are you called to repent? What does repentance mean to you?

Prayer for the Day
Lord, we struggle with knowing what messages are your word to us and what are the loud voices within and around us claiming to know best, but often leading us in the wrong direction. Quiet in us all the distractions that do not lead us closer to you. Give us the wisdom to discern rightly the instructions of your prophets, past and present. Do not let us judge solely on appearances but help us to carefully, prayerfully seek out the wisdom of those whose outward lives match their inward commitment to you. Amen.

Thursday

Mark 6:7–13

[Jesus] ordered them to take nothing for their journey except a staff; no bread, no bag, no money in their belts; but to wear sandals and not to put on two tunics.

Mark 6:8–9

Empty Belts

Sandwiched between Jesus' rejection from his hometown of Nazareth and the death of John the Baptist, the twelve disciples go out two by two into the world to preach, teach, heal, and cast out demons. How confident would they have been after having seen Jesus himself disrespected and subsequently unable to perform miracles among those who knew him best? And, by the way, do not take anything with you on this perilous journey where people may or may not welcome you. A contemporary reality show has nothing on first century discipleship. Go, tell people to repent, do not take food, a bag, or money. Be ready to depend on the hospitality of strangers. Do what you can to ease the suffering of those you encounter along the way.

When I consider the risks those first followers of Jesus took for his sake, I am humbled. Embarrassed, really. When have I done anything remotely similar? I get anxious when someone emails me their disapproval of the sermon or posts a less-than-affirming comment on social media. Jesus tells the people closest to him who have already left what they knew, family, friends, professions, community, to risk even more for the sake of the gospel. Do not even tuck a twenty in your belt in case of emergency, just head out and start telling and enacting the story of God's nearness and power.

Recently, in the wake of protests in response to yet another killing of an unarmed Black person by police, several close friends, awakened and stunned by the brutal, violent video of this murder, have asked me, "What do we do?" This question is oft repeated by well-intentioned people themselves not subject to daily fear of random brutality and centuries-long discrimination. I certainly have asked this question myself. We pose it in the face of a myriad of the world's problems. Poverty, war, illness, injustice: What do we do? However, too often we make this a rhetorical question, coupled with a shrug of the shoulders or a sigh of resignation. And yet, discipleship in the Gospels is anything but rhetorical or theoretical. Following Jesus is, in fact, literal, actual, physical. Faithfulness to God demands that we alter where we go, with whom we interact, and what we take on the journey.

Go. Proclaim. Teach. Heal. Cast out demons. Do not do this alone. Do not be weighed down by baggage, by the need to protect your possessions, your investment in worldly security. Radical trust in the One who sends you is needed because you are not to stuff your belt with all the things you think will keep you safe and apart from the pain of those you encounter along the way. Remember, Jesus got rejected by the people who raised him, and John the Baptist is about to get killed for his testimony. All right, head out to those people and places who need relief from oppression, poverty, illness, and all manner of suffering.

Sobering, isn't it? Discipleship should cause us to stop and wonder if we are ready to do what God calls us to do. We cannot ask in earnest, "What do we do?" if we are not prepared for the answer to require that we go with little more than the power of God and faith in Jesus Christ. Discipleship is anything but hypothetical. What are we willing to leave behind and take on to bear witness to the world that the gospel is actual and life-changing? What *will* we do?

Questions for Reflection
1. When you imagine going on a journey and not taking anything with you, what feelings does this engender? Why do you think Jesus tells the disciples to go in pairs and not take anything with them?
2. What have you left behind or taken on in response to Jesus' call?
3. When have you experienced an "empty belt"? Did you need to depend on others?

Prayer for the Day
Lord Christ, as we prepare to celebrate your incarnation, we listen now for your call. You leave the confines of heaven and come to earth a vulnerable infant. You experience the rejection from those you love and suffer the violence of the cross, sacrificing everything for our sake and the sake of the world. And

yet, we take our discipleship casually and think that we can choose when and how to obey your commandments. Forgive our flippant following and strengthen our faith so that we will go where you send us, leave behind what hinders our witness, and be free to enact your healing with those most in need of hearing good news. Amen.

Friday

John 21:15–19

"Very truly, I tell you, when you were younger, you used to fasten your own belt and to go wherever you wished. But when you grow old, you will stretch out your hands, and someone else will fasten a belt around you and take you where you do not wish to go."

John 21:18

Fasten Your Belt

Fast forward from Advent to Easter and Jesus gives Peter this sobering word. This declaration comes just after the question-and-answer period when Jesus repeatedly queries, "Do you love me?" and Peter emphatically replies, "Yes, Lord; you know that I love you." In between, Jesus instructs Peter, "Feed my sheep." Then there is this bit about Peter eventually being unable to dress himself. The writer of the Gospel gives us a parenthetical explanation about indicating the way Peter would die, but is this fate of dependency not universal for any of us who reach a ripe old age?

74

Why does Jesus call Peter to an awareness of his finitude? Why does Jesus give Peter a mission and then remind him that he will, at some point, lack agency and be reliant on others for even the most basic of tasks? Is Jesus letting Peter know that he will be imprisoned for the sake of the gospel or is this a more general declaration of human limitations? Both?

One of the gifts of ministry comes in the form of relationships with many who no longer fasten their own belts, who rely on others to dress, wash, and feed them. Once stalwart feeders and tenders of others come to a time when they must depend on others to do likewise for them. Few of them welcome this reality. Some are more accepting of it than others. Inevitably, they grieve the loss of control over much of what used to be routine. Depending on others, often on strangers, is a vulnerable and, at times, frightening reality.

One of my friends who resides in an assisted living facility knows when which staff members are working and subsequently who to ask for help in what areas and when to anticipate more or less care and compassion. Small kindnesses go a long way. He will tell me when someone positions his nightstand so that he has easier access to his cell phone or when the person delivering his breakfast tray brings an extra cup of coffee. I value my conversations with him because he is interesting and asks about me and my family despite his own challenges and needs. I appreciate his friendship because he gives me a needed perspective. I find myself grateful for that which I ordinarily dismiss. When he tells me about a nursing assistant who is kind and will take his time getting him dressed and out of bed, I get up and choose my clothing and fasten my own belt with a gratitude and recognition that such autonomy is not a given and not forever.

These last words Jesus utters in John come on the heels of instructions for his followers to show their love to him through feeding and tending others. Perhaps the two are intimately related because only when we remember that we too will be dependent on others to feed and tend us, will we feed and tend God's sheep with patience, kindness, and love. Jesus, our incarnate Savior, knows well our human vulnerability and he calls on his disciples to feed and tend others with that recognition always in the forefront of our minds. How we feed and tend reflects in whose name we care for one another.

Questions for Reflection

1. Why do you think Jesus tells Peter that he will eventually be unable to do as he chooses?
2. When have you been dependent upon another person for your care? How was that experience?
3. When have you been the caregiver? Was it challenging to tend and feed another or others?

Prayer for the Day

Incarnate God, Immanuel, you became fully human, taking on our vulnerability, becoming intimately aware of our finitude and fears. When you instruct us to feed and tend your sheep, you remind us that how we care for one another matters. We are called to be in relationship with each other, showing forth your compassion, mercy, and kindness in all of our interactions. Help us to depend on you as we seek to be dependable disciples, demonstrating our love for you in our love for your flock, ever mindful that even as we tend and feed your sheep, at some point others will feed and tend us. Amen.

Saturday

Revelation 1:9–16

Then I turned to see whose voice it was that spoke to me, and on turning I saw seven golden lampstands, and in the midst of the lampstands I saw one like the Son of Man, clothed with a long robe and with a golden sash across his chest.

Revelation 1:12–13

Golden Belt

How do you envision the risen and ascended Christ? We know what infants look like. We have seen infants up close. As we make ready for the baby Jesus, we might imagine what Mary and Joseph felt like as the time of his birth approached. We know what babies need and the feelings they engender in us when they cry or cannot be consoled or stretch us to our limits due to their demands and our lack of sleep. But as we prepare for the incarnation, the baby Jesus, do we also hold in our minds the reality that this child is also the risen and ascended Christ who sits at the right hand of God and will at some point return? Do we consider what John of Patmos' otherworldly picture of a powerful, golden-belted, white-haired, eyes-on-fire Christ has to say to our churches, to us, in our time?

It is easy to sentimentalize the baby Jesus. We can almost hear that familiar hymn about the little Lord Jesus no crying he makes, picture the pristine images of a serene holy family and a tidy stable. Our Savior gets domesticated and therefore controllable and safe. We tend to eliminate the messy realities of childbirth and caregiving. Infants control our waking and sleeping and, if we are a nursing mother, our very bodies. Though small, their influence and disruption impacts every aspect of the household they enter. So it should be for the infant Jesus in our lives.

John's vision of the Son of Man in Revelation reminds us to take this incarnate Savior with utter seriousness. John cannot remain on his feet in the face of such power and glory. No one who encounters the living God remains unmoved. And yet, for many of us the run up to Christmas is anything but awe-inspiring and spirit-arresting. We grow weary with capitalistic pressures, tired of fulfilling cultural, material expectations, exhausted, stressed, and stretched by the time we sing "Silent Night." We may well fall down as if dead, but not out of holy awe.

What if we looked to the end, to John's vision of the ascended Christ, even as we plan to welcome Jesus' earthly beginning? Could we remember that the infant Immanuel covered in swaddling clothes is also the glorious risen Christ wrapped in a golden belt? Would holding these two images of our Lord in tension remind us to never domesticate and control the One who comes to make all things new? The One who comes to upend our expectations and set God's will loose in the world? Our Savior who comes into our world right now reigns over all and will, in God's time, come again. Nothing is off-limits for Jesus' influence. Right now Immanuel, God with us, is also the One with the voice of many roaring waters, the Word made flesh with a living word for us, our churches, our towns. What does Jesus have to say to the angels of our churches? Do we have the ears to hear what the Spirit is saying to the churches?

Questions for Reflection

1. How do you picture Jesus as an infant? A grown man? Risen and ascended? Where do these images come from and what impact do they have on how you understand Jesus?
2. How do we domesticate and attempt to control Jesus in our culture?
3. Have you ever had an experience of the holy that upended your plans or expectations?

Prayer for the Day

Lord Christ, as we make ready for your birth, we do not want to forget that you sit at the right hand of God and reign over all. As we envision you as an infant, we also picture you in glory. We cannot control you, for you are Lord of everything. Recognizing your power and greatness, we bow down and worship, utterly speechless and humbled. In your mercy, you come to us, touch us, tell us to fear not, and show us through your incarnation what the Spirit is saying. Give us the ears to hear, right now, your word for us, our churches, our communities. Amen.

Fourth Week of Advent

Trees

Sunday

Genesis 2:4–9

Out of the ground the LORD God made to grow every tree that is pleasant to the sight and good for food, the tree of life also in the midst of the garden, and the tree of the knowledge of good and evil.

Genesis 2:9

The Tree of Life

God is good, all the time. This familiar refrain resounds through sanctuaries when the preacher and the congregation feel compelled to praise the Lord and affirm God's goodness regardless of present circumstances. The leader shouts, "God is good!" Those gathered respond, "All the time!" The leader then says, "All the time!" The congregation affirms, "God is good!" Being in the middle of an energetic group carried away with this proclamation buoys the spirit, energizes the soul, encourages faithful bravery in the face of all that attempts to defy God's goodness. Recognizing the foundational truth of divine goodness allows people of faith to call out evil and even dare to combat it with tenacious love.

From the beginning, the very beginning, the creation account beginning, God is good. God creates goodness. God's performative word names the goodness of all God makes. God's goodness is gratuitous, over-the-top, unnecessary. The Lord God made to grow every tree that is pleasant to the sight and good for food. Divine provisions move well beyond utilitarian and commerce in beauty. Walking through the woods or a city park or even driving on a busy interstate, the diversity and glory of God's work cannot be missed if one is open to looking up and out. When I look out my window, I see a dogwood tree, tall pines, stocky cedars, oaks, and redbuds. The other day, at the end of my driveway, I discovered thorny blackberry vines with their fruit in stages of red and dark purple. I planted none of these. I water none of these. These pleasant trees were here long before me and will remain long after I am gone. Their grandeur and utility put me in my place and grant needed perspective.

Seeing the glory, tenacity, longevity, variety of the trees that surround me reveals God's goodness, all the time, when I am awake enough to pay attention to them. The tree of life in Genesis exists not only in the garden of Eden, but in my backyard and indeed all over the world. God's good creation provides and sustains life, abundant life, not mere survival. Trees clean the air and water, they provide shade and produce fruit, they mark the seasons and time, and they are pleasant to the sight to boot. They are life-giving reflections of our life-giving God. They persistently dot the landscapes around us and remind us that God is good, all the time, all the time, God is good. God desires goodness, all the time, all the time, God desires goodness.

This season many of us will put up a tree within the walls of our homes, string it with lights, and decorate it with ornaments for no purpose other than to enjoy its super-fluous beauty. Why go through all the effort? What's the point? Perhaps we yearn to participate in God's creative, lovely, life-affirming, good creation in a way that defies whatever conspires to overtake the light and love of the One who sends Jesus Christ not to condemn the world but to save it. Maybe we, too, want to be over-the-top in our expressions of beauty that signal to those with eyes to see that God is good, all the time. All the time, God is good.

Questions for Reflection

1. What reminds you of God's goodness? Is there something in creation that reminds you of God's good and life-giving presence?
2. During this Advent season, when we are called to be awake to God, what is giving you a sense of God's nearness to you?
3. Could your prayer today be the call and response, "God is good, all the time"? How does repeating this truth color your perspective?

Prayer for the Day

God you are good, all the time. Your goodness resounds through creation and through every creature. You gift us with beauty so diverse and persistent that were we to notice all of it, we would be utterly overwhelmed by your life-affirming power. As we go about our day, grant us eyes to see the trees of life that surround us, giving thanks for their ability to provide food, shelter for animals, air for us to breathe, leaves and flowers that are breathtakingly pleasing to our sight. All the time, you, God, are good. Help us to recognize your goodness and make it visible to others. Amen.

Monday

Psalm 1

They are like trees
planted by streams of water,
which yield their fruit in its season,
and their leaves do not wither.
In all that they do, they prosper.
                                    Psalm 1:3

The Tree by the Stream

Those who delight in the law of the Lord, they are like trees planted by streams of living water. Those who delight in God's ways have access always to that which enlivens and refreshes. In contrast, the psalmist writes, are those who follow the advice of the wicked. Seems a stark choice, does it not? A clear choice, really. Of course, I will pick God's law over the advice of the wicked. Of course, we would like to think we would delight in God's instructions rather than heed the word of the wicked. And yet, the will to relish God's teachings often gets overwhelmed by the magnitude and volume of the world's less-than-holy messages.

Consider how many advertisements you see in a day. They pop up on your computer, encroach on your entertainment, scream at you from highway billboards, talk to you from the gas pump, interrupt your music listening. Each one is calculated to persuade you to buy something that you need to be whole or beautiful or important. Add to this barrage the endless pundits, commentators, and experts, each offering the inside line on what they say is true, wise, and needful of your attention. Then there are those in your life, friends, mentors, pastors, family members, coworkers, some of whom you trust and admire greatly, each with their own perspective on what is good and right and what is bad and wrong. We also must contend with the running commentary in our own minds, opinions, unconscious biases, long-held assumptions, unexamined ideas, and random thoughts. Where, in all of this, is God's law? God's word? God's teachings?

Of course, we want to delight in God's law and be planted by a stream of living water, bearing beautiful, nurturing fruit for all the world to witness, but the distractions and contradictions and confusion as to what God says are myriad. Seasons such as this one invite us to intentionally tune our senses to God's law and God's word to us, to attend to where we plant ourselves and what takes root in and around us as a result. If we are to be those sheltering, fruit-bearing trees in this world, we must do more than know God's law, we must delight in it so much we seek it out and embody it.

Trees planted by streams take up the water to which they are adjacent, they become one with that which sustains them. Imagine if this were so of us as we reveled in

God's living Word? What allows you proximity to that stream of God's commandments and teaching? Bible study with trusted disciples of different backgrounds and experiences? Daily reading of Scripture? Worship? I find prayer walks that include guided meditation, often ones punctuated with Bible verses, help me to tune into the signal of God's voice despite all the chaotic noise around me. After a walk, I find God's Word coming unbidden to my consciousness throughout the day. I notice birds flying overhead and think, "Consider the ravens," and I am reminded to be not anxious, even for just a moment. I see the discarded water bottle on the ground and I hear Jesus' words, "Out of the believer's heart shall flow rivers of living water" (John 7:38) and remember that God will equip those whom God calls. Each moment of awareness of God's law speaks of God's presence, grants perspective, enables me access to God's power and is, well, delightful.

Questions for Reflection

1. When have you felt like a tree planted by a stream, nurtured, strong, and fruitful? What contributed to this feeling?
2. When, in contrast, have you felt depleted, empty, and in need of renewal, rest? What contributed to this state?
3. How do you delight in God's law and tune out the advice of the wicked? What practices enable you to do this better?

Prayer for the Day

Lord, your law is delightful. You give us commandments and instructions so that we might experience the abundant life Christ came to bring. Your limits are not meant to punish us, but rather enable us to be truly free, to be the people you created us to be. As we travel through this Advent journey, help us to plant ourselves firmly in your Word as we prepare for the coming of the Word made flesh. Do not let the advice of the wicked overtake our delight in your law. Grant us daily your living water so that we will not thirst and will bear fruit in your name. Amen.

Tuesday

Job 14:1–10

"For there is hope for a tree,
if it is cut down, that it will sprout again,
and that its shoots will not cease."

Job 14:7

Felled Trees

I learned a new word the other day: coppicing. I was watching a documentary that featured ancient wooden bowls crafted from tree stumps, trees that had been coppiced. Curious as to what the term meant, I went to Google, where Wikipedia informed me that, "Coppicing is a traditional method of woodland management which exploits the capacity of many species of trees to put out new shoots from their stump or roots if cut down. In a coppiced wood, which is called a copse, young tree stems are repeatedly cut down to near ground level, resulting in a stool."* The

*"Coppicing." *Wikipedia*, Wikimedia Foundation, en.wikipedia.org/wiki /Coppicing#.

entry went on to say that forests maintained in this way keep trees at a juvenile stage so that they never die of old age therefore, ironically, often reach "immense ages." Perhaps Job knew this method of woodland management as he contrasted human finitude with trees' immortality. Since God "has appointed bounds that they cannot pass" (v. 5), our days are literally numbered, but there is hope for the tree, cut to the stump in order that exponential new growth will come and, as it does, wildlife flourishes all around the stool.

What do we make of this stark difference between trees and human beings? Job, of course, has reasons to lament finitude, death, and the real limits of our power and longevity. But is there more to his comparison than despair? Is there, in fact, hope in knowing that our days on earth will not last forever? One night after a long day, a grief-infused day, a day when I had run up against the brick wall of my inability to intervene on behalf of my loved one in any way that felt useful, I drove home tired and defeated. As I made my way on a familiar highway, it appeared to my right so bright that for a disorienting moment, I thought I saw the sun setting even though it was well after dark. As I rounded a corner, there appeared a huge, unbelievably bright, full moon. So luminous was the moon and so cloudless the sky, day and night seemed to strangely merge. The trees along the highway were no longer outlines, but visible in detail against the horizon. One or two cars crossed my path, but otherwise I felt alone, a dot on the landscape of creation. I felt an unmistakable sense of God's presence.

In that moment, rather than feeling sad at my smallness, I felt hope in the trees, in the moon, in the vastness that existed well before me and would persist long after my determined days ended. Is this how Job felt? Did he, in all he had lived through and lost, find comfort in the grandeur and relentlessness of God's good universe? Out of felled trees come shoots that do not cease. From that copse that appears dead and gone, comes life that nurtures more life that never dies. Knowing our finitude and creation's fecundity helps us not only count our days, but treasure them, reminds us that we are precious in God's sight, every hair on our heads counted, and yet a minuscule part of God's beloved world. The felled tree that brings forth new shoots reminds us, too, not to give in to hopelessness, because it may be that not only trees experience coppicing, but we do as well. As those who follow a Savior who spent his days working with the wood from felled trees, we can trust that within our losses and limits God is at work crafting something beautiful, knowing the coppicing makes of us and the landscapes around us new creations.

Questions for Reflection

1. Have you experienced a sense of awe and wonder in creation? Where were you? Did you sense God's presence?
2. When you think of our human boundedness and finitude, what feelings emerge? How are our limits both a challenge and a gift?
3. Literally or metaphorically, when have you seen new growth from what appeared to be a lifeless landscape?

Prayer for the Day

Creator God, teach us to number our days so that we will not take them for granted but instead rejoice in the gift of this life, in all its twists and turns, challenges and beauty. When we despair at the state of the world or the pain of our personal

*circumstances, help us to look to the hope of the trees, the vast-
ness of the universe for perspective, the persistence of new life
in nature that reminds us that you continue to work for good
around and within us. We give thanks that within our finitude
your grace and hope is made known to us. Amen.*

Wednesday

Isaiah 41:8–20

I will put in the wilderness the cedar,
  the acacia, the myrtle, and the olive;
I will set in the desert the cypress,
  the plane and the pine together,
so that all may see and know,
  all may consider and understand,
that the hand of the LORD has done this,
  the Holy One of Israel has created it.
      Isaiah 41:19–20

Trees in the Wilderness

Fear not, for I am with you. This poetic selection of verses details God's powerful, sure providing for God's people. Protection. Food. Water. Safety. Security. God declares, "I will strengthen you, I will help you, I will uphold you with my victorious right hand" (v. 10). All to the end that the world will see and know that the Lord has done these miraculous things. The striking trees, growing in the wilderness, could only exist as a result of God's doing. No human could ever create such a forest in such a place. See and know, consider and understand, sustenance in the desert is God's loving purview. How will we live in response?

Some translations include the word "together" in verse twenty, "consider and understand together" it reads. The seeing and knowing, the considering and understanding, the inspecting and perceiving of the meaning of the wilderness trees should be done as a community; all are to participate in this recognition of God's creating and doing. The "you" in these verses is plural. God is strengthening God's people, not only individuals within it. Often, in our American culture, we miss this critical point, while each person is a beloved member of the body, God's concern and care encompasses the whole and is for the sake of all.

Frankly, I do not know a cedar from a myrtle, or an oak from an acacia. It would be easy for me to dismiss the remarkable feat of such trees growing in the wilderness. I could assume, given my lack of knowledge, that such a landscape is unremarkable—lovely, but not miraculous. I need others to help me rightly see and know, consider and understand, the divine at work in wilderness places. Sometimes I cannot see the holy trees for the cluttered forest of life. When we survey the places around us, contemplate contemporary events and past experiences, we only truly perceive God's creative doing when we ponder them together.

In the midst of the pandemic, when chaos and fear were ever-present, I met online with a group of trusted colleagues, all of us wrestling with how to do and be church and so much more. Fatigue and worry evident on the faces in the little boxes on the screen, one member of the groups said after a moment or two, "I have seen remarkable things happen." She went on to detail people stepping up to care for each other, sacrificial giving to help those hit hard economically, those previously unable to participate in worship present at every online gathering. Her seeing and perception prompted each of us to notice God's creating in the middle of this unwanted, unexpected, and vast desert time. Family dinners now that all the kids' events no longer crowded the calendar. Reconnecting with old friends. An appreciation of simple pleasures. A sense of increased purpose and commitment to caring for essential but heretofore undervalued workers. Cedars, acacia, myrtles, and olives, trees in the wilderness, God's provisions, we would have missed had we not considered and understood the landscape together.

Questions for Reflection

1. When have you experienced God's provisions? When have you taken them for granted or missed them altogether?
2. Have you experienced a time when considering and seeing with others enabled you to know and understand something you would have otherwise not perceived?
3. What trees have grown in the wilderness of your life?

Prayer for the Day

God, you tell us to fear not because you are with us, at work among us, always providing for the world you created and love. Often when we survey the landscapes of our lives we focus on what is missing rather than the countless good gifts we need only to receive. When we get overwhelmed by the dangers of the wilderness, help us to come together with others so that we can rightly perceive your loving care, even and especially in the places that feel most threatening and frightening. Thank you for the cedars and acacia, the myrtles and olives, the cypress, plane and pine, miraculously growing in the most unexpected of places. Amen.

Thursday

Matthew 3:7–12

"Even now the ax is lying at the root of the trees; every tree therefore that does not bear good fruit is cut down and thrown into the fire."

Matthew 3:10

The Axe at the Root of the Tree

We cannot escape John the Baptist's brutally honest admonitions in Advent. Just as the world is singing cheering songs of Santa and jingle bells, John the Baptist calls us all a brood of vipers and warns us that right now the ax is lying at the root of the trees: bear good fruit or else! The juxtaposition jars us on days when we ache to hear beloved Christmas carols and instead get brooding Advent hymns. We want "Joy to the World." We get "Day of Wrath! That Day of Burning." What gives? Why the harsh word in a season of twinkling lights? Why a threat of destruction in this supposedly most wonderful time of the year?

John the Baptist and his call to prepare for the coming Messiah refuses to let us do so without utter seriousness and honest self-examination. No cheap grace here. No overlooking our real need for a Savior. No imagining that even if we wear all the religious trappings of righteousness, even if we follow all the holy rituals, that our lives really show forth the love and will of the God who comes to bring release to the captives and good news to the poor. None of us can presume we have a pass to go to the front of the line when Jesus comes. None of us can presume we get a gold star in faithfulness. God knows the heart. Jesus inspects the fruit we bear, not the titles we use or the beliefs we voice.

A wise and thoughtful friend, who happens to be a psychiatrist, gave me sage advice, "Listen to what people say. Believe what they do." Jesus, too, believes what we do or what we fail to do. As we make ready for his earthly arrival, how do our words and actions match or conflict? When he surveys the terrain of our lives, our bank statements, social media posts, interactions with strangers and family, the ways and places we exert our time and energy and influence, what trees are barren, fruitless, good for nothing but fire fodder?

In his book *You Are What You Love: The Spiritual Power of Habit*, James K.A. Smith argues that we are what we love and we may not love what we think we love. He encourages us to do a liturgical audit of our lives. He writes,

> Look at your daily, weekly, monthly, annual routines. What are the things you do that do something *to* you? What are the secular liturgies in your life? What vision of the good life is carried in those liturgies? What Story is embedded in those cultural practices? What kind of person do they want you to become?*

*James K.A. Smith, *You Are What You Love: The Spiritual Power of Habit* (Grand Rapids: Brazos, 2016), 55.

John the Baptist refuses to let us welcome Jesus without first carefully preparing, examining the topography of our lives and doing serious pruning of those trees that we may love, but that do not bear fruit. We cannot presume that we love what we say we love. We need to be fruit inspectors, taking note of when our words and our actions do not match up. Now is our opportunity to repent and welcome Jesus' refining fire.

Questions for Reflection

1. Do you find John the Baptist incongruous with the cultural Christmas season? Why do you think John the Baptist is an important character and message during Advent?
2. Do you love what you think you love? Pay attention for a day or more to how you spend your resources, all of them. What do they reveal about what you love?
3. When you survey the landscape of your life, are there fruitless trees that need to be cut down and thrown into the fire?

Prayer for the Day

Dear God, you send messengers to help us prepare for the coming of our Savior. They come in odd garb, proclaiming words we do not always welcome. We do not want to see ourselves among that brood of vipers and yet we know there is much in our lives that does not resemble your ways. As we make ready for Immanuel, grant us the courage to see rightly where our words and deeds do not match. When we repent and turn toward you, you are merciful and eager to forgive. Take our barren trees and turn them into a burning fire that points to Jesus Christ. Amen.

Friday

Matthew 7:15–20

You will know them by their fruits. Are grapes gathered from thorns, or figs from thistles? In the same way, every good tree bears good fruit, but the bad tree bears bad fruit.
Matthew 7:16–17

Good Trees

Discernment: such a churchy word. Often discernment gets thrown around when someone does not want to commit in the moment to a request or obligation. "Would you teach the Wednesday night Bible study?" "Well, let me pray about it and discern if God is calling me to that service." It could also be applied to major life decisions like a job change or career path or relationship status. Rarely do we discern our dinner plans or which route to take to work. Those are merely decisions, not cause for discernment. I wonder, however, if our discerning is misguided and if we might rather think of ourselves as keen observers, rather than dogged discerners. I think we ought to be more expansive in our search for the divine. The incarnation shows us without question that God enters fully all our humanness and nothing is therefore off-limits to God.

Advent offers us a season to hone our holy watching and take notice of where the good fruit grows and where, on the other hand, poisonous fruit lurks. This text from Matthew warns disciples to be on the lookout for false prophets that look like sheep on the outside, but beneath that gentle, warm exterior, are ravenous wolves. Examine carefully not just the outward appearance of those claiming to be and do good, but inspect their actual behavior and hold it up to the person and commandments of Jesus Christ.

Sadly, church history, ancient and contemporary, shows all too starkly that wolves in sheep's clothing often claim to be prophets, pastors, priests, and attentive volunteers, their victims injured badly in the name of the Lord. Our vigilance for good and bad fruit helps protect the most vulnerable, and while judgment is always coupled with mercy, grace, and forgiveness, it never should be exercised at the expense of those injured.

False prophets abound, often undetected when we neglect the spiritual discipline of prayerful, intentional attentiveness to the fruits being borne from the trees all around us. One of my trusted colleagues in my local Charlottesville, Virginia, clergy group monitors the social media and web activities of white supremacist groups and their leaders. I am not sure I have the fortitude of faith for such a task. He observes toxic fruit that turns the stomach. His willingness to enter those spaces is a ministry of great service as he informs us when danger is lurking, often posing as sheep. Before we gather for a community worship service marking the tragic August 2017 events in our town, he shares photos of white supremacists with the potential to show up and cause harm. He informs those of us whose names and towns are on lists being posted on neo-Nazi websites so that we can be aware and take prudent steps in response. One photo he shared sticks in my mind: a young man wearing a T-shirt emblazoned with "Believer, John 3:16." That shirt does not match the vitriol on his social media posts calling for the Confederate government to be reinstalled. While I pray for this person, I also pray the people of his faith community are fruit inspectors, willing to speak the truth in love in the hope that their holy observing will help facilitate a divine intervention.

Questions for Reflection
1. How do we practice holy watching and exercise judgment with a spirit of love and grace?
2. What is the end goal of detecting false prophets? How can that end shape how we go about this fruit inspection?
3. False prophets do not readily look like false prophets; what is the good and bad fruit we are to be on the lookout for when discerning to whom we should listen and who we should follow?

Prayer for the Day
Lord, you tell us to judge not lest we be judged. Yet, you also admonish us to be on the lookout for false prophets in our midst. We struggle with how to follow both of these instructions. We know, too, our tendency to call out the speck in another's eye while not noticing the log in our own. Nonetheless, we recognize that your disciples are obligated to protect the weak and vulnerable, to seek to restore the lost, to work to tend good, life-giving fruit in ourselves and in those around us. We ask for wisdom, humility, and eyes to see rightly those whom we should emulate and those whom we ought to refute. Help us to speak the truth in love. Amen.

Saturday

Matthew 13:31–32

[Jesus] put before them another parable: "The kingdom of heaven is like a mustard seed that someone took and sowed in his field; it is the smallest of all the seeds, but when it has grown it is the greatest of shrubs and becomes a tree, so that the birds of the air come and make nests in its branches."

Matthew 13:31–32

The Biggest of Trees

Jesus tells many parables about the kingdom of heaven, rich metaphors that unveil God's character and values. "The kingdom of heaven is like . . ." Jesus says over and over again. The kingdom of heaven is like leaven, like a net cast into the sea, like a treasure hidden in the sea, and a king who throws a wedding banquet for his son, and often, repeatedly, like some sort of seed and sowing. The Savior of the world who enters this world as an infant in a powerless family, proclaims that God operates through ordinary things and everyday events.

The kingdom of heaven is like a mustard seed, tiny, easily overlooked, yet capable in the right conditions of producing a sizable tree that provides shelter for the birds of the air. God works relentlessly, often unnoticed, to provide places of shelter and nurture for creatures big and small. God's realm entails utilizing the common and the insignificant in life-giving ways that defy expectation and human imagination. What if we really believed that the kingdom of heaven, present even now on earth, is like a tiny mustard seed that explodes in growth and spreads exponentially, invading the landscapes all around us in order to create places of relief and protection and care and joy? Like mustard-seed-sized faith that Jesus says can move mountains, mustard-seed-sized compassion can change communities, mustard-seed-sized forgiveness can restore societies, mustard-seed-sized mercy can heal families, mustard-seed-sized justice can reorder cultures.

The kingdom of heaven is like a mustard seed, that tiniest of seeds, that when it grows—and grow it will because it is like an invasive species, not a delicate cutting—it cannot be ignored, it overflows with all kinds of birds, making nests, making noise, producing more life. What if we embraced this truth and lived it, boldly? Imagine if we began to spread little gospel mustard seeds with prayerful hope that God would give them the growth? Perhaps we could start with a vision of the large, glorious trees we want to see all around the globe. What kinds of redwood-like forests do we want to grow? How lush a rainforest can we allow ourselves to envision?

I would want to see a verdant, abundant swath of early childhood education for every child, all the children Jesus says he welcomes and the ones we are not to turn away from him. And what about a forest of strong, sturdy oaks of accessible health care that fosters wholeness of body, mind, and spirit? I envision a society of good neighbors and good neighborhoods where people enjoy one another's company and celebrate their differences and make sure everyone has enough. I want to see people housed and paid a living wage and the earth tended for the sake of future generations—not exploited for the sake of quarterly profits. What big, life-giving, nurturing, sheltering, beautiful trees do you long to sit under in your community? In God's beloved world? What if we started planting the mustard-sized seeds that God can grow into them?

Questions for Reflection

1. When you hear parables about the kingdom of heaven, what does the phrase "kingdom of heaven" mean to you?
2. What are the big trees you want to see grow in your life? Community? What small seeds can you sow that God can use to grow into them?
3. Notice the big trees all around you today and remember that they had small beginnings. What feelings or thoughts does that reality bring up for you?

Prayer for the Day

Lord of mustard seeds and leaven, lost coins and hidden treasure, we marvel at your power to bring forth abundant life from such common and small things. When we despair at our lack of resources or our uncertainty about the state of our hearts or the scale of the world's problems, remind us that we are saved through Jesus Christ, who came to earth as a vulnerable infant, called ordinary people as disciples, died on a cross and now, raised from the dead, is Lord of all. In that sure knowledge we ask only to be bold in sowing mustard-sized gospel seeds, trusting you will bring the growth. Amen.

Christmas Eve: Cloth

Luke 2:1–7

And she gave birth to her firstborn son and wrapped him in bands of cloth, and laid him in a manger, because there was no place for them in the inn.

Luke 2:7

Swaddling Clothes

My Bible dictionary tells me that wrapping an infant in bands of cloth is "a normal act of childcare for warmth, security, etc." I like the "etc." included in the definition of *sparganoo*. Even the person who put together the entry in the reference resource recognizes that swaddling a baby, while practical and soothing, also entails an ineffable more. I picture Mary, exhausted from her trip and from childbirth, taking each strip of cloth and tenderly wrapping it around her firstborn son. I wonder if she did so haltingly, unsure if she was getting it right.

I remember attempting to swaddle my firstborn a few hours after his birth. The nurse unwrapped the sleeping bundle, so snug and content, quickly gave me a demonstration, and invited me to give it a try. It looked so easy. It proved to be more complicated in practice. What she had made look neat and secure, I managed to make look like a lumpy mess from which my son's head was barely visible. His little legs kicked, he flailed his arms inside the spacious sack and started to cry. The experienced nurse swooped over, unrolled the flannel blanket and within seconds had him looking once again like a fuzzy, pale blue burrito in a knit cap. Instantly, his crying ceased. She handed me my baby and assured me I would master the swaddling technique soon enough.

Consoled and awake, his bright eyes stared up at me. Stunned he existed, was present in my arms, dependent upon me to care for him, I wondered about the wisdom of these competent people allowing me to take him home mere hours after his arrival. I realized the preparation classes, the ones in which we diapered and swaddled a doll, did not cover all of the "etc." of childcare. Nonetheless, our family of three drove out of the hospital parking lot unsupervised the next day.

The miracle is that I did learn to swaddle him in cloth, as did my husband. We learned how to comfort him, what eased his stress, and what exacerbated his discomfort. We rocked him and walked with him, paced really, his little head in the palm of his father's hand, his body resting on Grant's forearm as Grant bounced him gently and sang Grateful Dead songs. We began to figure out the "etc." of loving someone more than we had previously known we could love another.

On Christmas Eve, the full humanness of Jesus stuns me no less than when I looked at my own firstborn. After all this waiting and a preparation that cannot really prepare us: he is finally here and oh-so-beloved. Mary wraps him in bands of cloth, for warmth, security, comfort, and so much more. Mary swaddles the baby in whom we will be clothed, all of us enveloped by the unrelenting compassion and grace of our God. Even as we stumble and bumble, learn and fail, nothing can undo the mantle of love in which we are covered. We see the baby Jesus wrapped by his mother in bands of cloth and know the One she holds has the whole world in his hands; therefore we can rest secure.

Questions for Reflection

1. What are your most vivid Christmas Eve memories? What do they mean to you?
2. Have you ever swaddled a baby? Does this image speak to you of God's love for us?
3. Whenever you touch cloth today, allow it to remind you that you are clothed in Christ, wrapped in the love of God. What might that feel like?

Prayer for the Day

Immanuel, God with us, our wait is over, you are here. When we picture you, wrapped in bands of cloth, resting in your mother's arms, we marvel that you came to us so humbly, without any earthly status. You truly are fully human, intimately aware of what it means to rely on others for care, to depend on people for help, to cry and hurt, to laugh and grow. You have compassion for us because you empathize with our vulnerability. As we celebrate your birth, we rejoice that we are enveloped in your love no less than you were swaddled in the manger. Amen.

Christmas Day: Light

John 1:1–5

The light shines in the darkness, and the darkness did not overcome it.

John 1:5

Abiding Light

In recent years, the world has felt very dark. Millions stricken with a relentless virus; millions struggling to make ends meet, many of them failing to do so and wondering how they will pay their rent, feed their children, get the medical care they need; natural disasters seemingly ever present; violence both local and between nations refuses to relent. Sadly, the previous sentence could be written on any day in any decade. The particulars change, the people inflicted are different, but the suffering remains. Sin, evil, and our creaturely limits remain, generation after generation. Our need for the light no darkness can overcome does not ever go away. The coming of Immanuel does not alter our immediate circumstances so much as upend how we navigate and understand them.

Just yesterday, driving home from a brief trip with family, I saw a billboard with these words emblazoned upon it: "Jesus is the answer to ALL your problems." I cannot say its sentiment engendered warm feelings in me. I wondered how non-Christians would read it, assuming it was erected as a form of highway evangelism. What bothered me about it was the transactional nature of it, the instrumentalism it expressed, the idea that Jesus is simply a means to an end or a magic bullet in the face of life's vicissitudes. It also felt like judgment upon my own sorrow regarding the current state of the world and a few personal challenges too. Was I not relying on Jesus enough? Do I not really love my Lord? Do I simply lack faith?

I could not shake my discomfort with the statement long after it was in my rearview mirror, my mood darkening with each passing mile. I drove through a torrential rainstorm that added to my sense of foreboding. Then, hours later, I rounded a corner and right before my eyes a rainbow arched through the clear, blue sky, an unmistakable sign of God's promise. Another hour passed and the sun began to set and oranges and purples streaked across the horizon. More time passed and a huge, luminous moon appeared, its presence unyielding and more and more obvious as darkness descended. Light present from the beginning that continues to shine and cannot be overcome.

Jesus, yes, helps me in my problems, provides hope, strength, and courage for the living of this hour. More than the answer, however, he is Immanuel, God with us, God for us, the Savior of the world who knows our human suffering and refuses to turn away from it, but instead endures it so that none of what we face is unknown or off-limits to God's grace. The One born this day does not provide us with answers so much as he remains with us and guides us as we wrestle with the most perplexing of life's questions. While we may want the clarity of a billboard, Jesus, the light of the world, offers us the unexpected beauty of a rainbow, the ever-changing colors of a sunset and the steady, relentless, unmistakable presence of a full moon, reminders of God's saving grace that nothing can overtake.

Questions for Reflection:

1. When have you been reminded of God's light in the midst of darkness? What were those literal or metaphorical light sources for you?
2. What does Christmas mean to you? How will you mark this day in ways that strengthen your relationship with Jesus?
3. When have you wanted a billboard, but gotten a rainbow instead? How did that sign help you at that time?

Prayer for the Day

Immanuel, you are indeed here with us. We waited and hoped, prepared and sometimes despaired, but nothing would prevent your coming to us. When we fear the darkness around us or within us will prevail, we remember today and know that truly nothing can separate us from God's love. Your light shines through the cracks and broken places, in the middle of the night, after the storms and with every sunrise. When we wonder where you are or if you are present, help us to see the light that cannot be overcome and illumine our path with it so that no matter what we can remain steadfast on your way. Amen.

First Week of Christmas

Hearts

Sunday

Isaiah 35:1–4

Say to those who are of a fearful heart,
  "Be strong, do not fear!
Here is your God.
  The Lord will come with vengeance,
with terrible recompense.
  God will come and save you."

Isaiah 35:4 alt.

Fearful Heart

Restoration, radical restoration resounds through these words from Isaiah. Those with fearful hearts need not remain terrified, soon God will come and set all things right. This is a proleptic text, one that describes and anticipates a future not yet here, but certain to come. Hard as it is to believe, the desert will overflow with flowers, those places so barren now will surely teem with life. Advent reminds us repeatedly that God is on the move, doing new, good, restorative, redemptive things. The challenge for those of us trudging through deserts of sorrow, pain, and confusion, those of us making our way through hard seasons or the daily grind, is to quell the fear in our hearts that such transformation is impossible.

We who follow the God of incarnation and new creation are called to move through this world anticipating divine intervention that works for good. We are to live proleptic lives, envisioning blooms in the desert and acting accordingly. I confess, such a hopeful, holy-leaning perspective does not come easily to me. I tend to get overwhelmed with the vastness of suffering, the seemingly endless swaths of deserts, so that my heart grows more fearful rather than strong. It takes effort to imagine desolate places rife with joy, strained relationships close again, broken institutions functional, oppressive structures upended and replaced. And yet, this is what the prophet Isaiah proclaims, this kind of revolutionary change is what we should expect this liturgical season.

We are a people of prolepsis, living into the not-yet but sure-to-come justice and peace of God. Andre Henry says of Jesus turning water into wine at the wedding at Cana that Jesus "invited them to partake of the world to come in the world that is. In social movement language, we call this 'prefigurative' action, where people seek to create a tiny microcosm of the world that ought to be in the middle of the world as we know it."* Such glimpses of the world as it ought to be make bold fearful hearts and begin to enact God's future in the present.

Perhaps a simpler way to look at this comes from the mouth of a child. My daughter babysits a little boy who just turned five. The other afternoon he was drawing

---

*Andre Henry, "When Christians won't acknowledge racism, protest becomes church," Religious News Service, June 8, 2020. https://religion news.com/2020/06/08/when-christians-wont-acknowledge-racism-protest -becomes-church/.

a picture and my daughter said, "That's really good. Are you going to be an artist when you grow up?" He paused, looked at her, and said, "I already am an artist." And, indeed, he is. Perhaps we could be more child-like, as Jesus tells us we need to be to enter the kingdom of heaven. Maybe this Advent we could practice "prefigurative action" and proleptic thinking. We already are redeemed. We already are saved. We already are courageous of heart and bold in faith. We already are children of God. We already are fishers of people. We already are makers of peace. We already are doers of justice, lovers of kindness, those who walk humbly with God. I feel my fearful heart becoming emboldened already.

Questions for Reflection

1. What makes your heart fearful? What alleviates those fears?
2. Can you think proleptically, living as if God's promised future is already present? What difference does such thinking make in how you feel and act?
3. Where do you right now see glimpses of the world as it ought to be?

Prayer for the Day

Alpha and Omega, God of our beginning, end and middle, while we cannot know what tomorrow holds, we know you have plans for our future, plans for the future of your beloved world. We know Jesus Christ will reveal your will for abundant life, radical restoration, and salvation for creation. Embolden our fearful hearts so that we can offer others a glimpse of your good future, right here on earth. Make of us embodied examples of blooms in the desert, wherever we are planted, signs that your new creation is surely coming and present even now. Amen.

Monday

Luke 2:8–20

But Mary treasured all these words and pondered them in her heart.

Luke 2:19

Pondering Heart

Mary listened as the shepherds shared all they had been told about her infant and while the others gathered wondered about these grand statements, Mary treasured them and pondered them in her heart. No doubt, as Jesus grew, Mary would return to the shepherds' proclamation and that of Gabriel's before them. God's calling and all that call entails remains a mystery, no matter how long one lives into it. When raising the Son of God got complicated and painful, when Jesus went missing as an adolescent or when he began to get in trouble with the authorities, Mary must have pondered in her heart all the more, mulling over treasured up words to reassure her of her son's well-being despite all the danger his mission engendered.

Like Mary, some of our lives' twists and turns, divine messages and earthly suffering, bring forth pondering in our hearts, an ongoing conversation between us and the God we long to trust but worry we might have misheard. When we attempt to heed God's call, to be faithful and step into a space we think God told us to go, one fraught with pain and upheaval, we need those treasured up words to ponder in order to remain steadfast. When our marriage gets rocky, we need to ponder in our heart the vows we made on our wedding day. When our beloved child becomes a rebellious teen, we need to ponder in our heart all the times this same child shared her affection without embarrassment. When the labor of love becomes drudgery, we call on saved up past experiences of joy and transformation and ponder them as a means of remembering why we got into this work in the first place.

We learn from Mary to pay attention when God speaks, whether through angels or shepherds. We learn from Mary to treasure up those holy moments of God's inbreaking. We learn from Mary to ponder in our heart the mysteries of God's call so that we can return to it when we worry we may have lost our way.

My road to ordination was not without twists, turns, detours, and dead ends. I started seminary, left, returned, did a few years of graduate school after seminary prior to being ordained and working in a local church. I questioned mightily God's call to ministry, avoided it for a while, bargained with God a good bit before finally, at least partially, saying, "Let it be with me according to your will." Such back and forth between human beings and God can be found throughout the biblical record. Moses thinks he does not speak well enough. Jeremiah attempts to keep God's word under wraps but it burns in his bones until he speaks. The disciples follow but fail to understand Jesus and his way repeatedly. I suspect even Mary makes a misstep in her child-rearing from time to time. Nonetheless, God's call persists, God's words, once spoken to us, cannot be unheard, once written on our hearts, we treasure them, ponder them, return to them and, with the help of the Holy Spirit, act on them.

Questions for Reflection

1. When have you heard God's voice? How was it communicated to you? How did you discern that it was God speaking?
2. When you think of God's call to you, what comes to mind? What word of the Lord to you do you treasure? Ponder in your heart?
3. Have you had times in your life of faith when you questioned God's providence? What words of God sustained you during that time?

Prayer for the Day

God of angels and shepherds, you speak to us in a multitude of ways, always seeking us out and coming to us to enlist us in your work and ways. We cannot fathom your mysteries, the depth of your love for the world, the relentlessness with which you work for good. And yet, you call us to participate in embodying your will, furthering your grace, and nurturing your compassion. Help us to treasure up your words and ponder in our hearts the Word made flesh, Jesus Christ, so that when we wonder what to do or where you are or how you are at work, we will remember your call to us and be at peace. Amen.

Tuesday

Psalm 51

Create in me a clean heart, O God,
and put a new and right spirit within me.
Psalm 51:10

Clean Heart

Create in me a clean heart, O God. This psalm of confession acknowledges that we need God to act upon us. We need God to cleanse us and set us right. We do, however, have a role in getting to this right disposition with God and it begins with recognizing our need for God to cleanse and set us right. This psalm is characterized by honest confession, humility, knowledge that our lives do not reflect God's will and character. We think of this psalm more with Ash Wednesday than with the season of Christmas, but reflecting on our sin against God in the wake of the incarnation invites us to a level of honesty commensurate with the revelation that Jesus came to save sinners. We can lay bare all of our heart and hold nothing back from the mercy of God evident in the coming of the Messiah.

Acknowledging our need for God to act, to cleanse our hearts and set us right, and seeing unequivocally that through Jesus Christ, God does act to put a right spirit within us, that nothing will or can separate us from the love of God, frees us to pour out our heart and soul without fear to the God who loves us. Imagine for a moment, telling God absolutely anything, absolutely everything on your heart and mind, those things of which you are ashamed, those actions or words you wish you could take back, those temptations into which you have given and those feelings that keep you awake at night. Jesus Christ came not to condemn the world but to save it. Hold nothing back, pour out your heart to the God who loves you enough to send the only Son to redeem all creation.

Can we embrace the truth that God has the ability and the will to cleanse our hearts, put a new and right spirit within us, to forgive and free us? One of the failures of our Christian imagination is embracing this truth and living out of it, both individually and as a communal force in society. We who should most embody the mercy of our Savior, we who should forgive as we have been forgiven, we who are to be engaged in the ministry of repair and reconciliation, often tout retribution and even revenge. We fail to believe the gospel promise that transformation is not only possible, it is inevitable and enacted with the birth of Jesus Christ.

If only just for today, pour out your heart to God. Hold nothing back and then rest in the truth that God cleanses that very heart, God, merciful and abounding in steadfast love, puts an entire new spirit within you. Behold, God is making all things new, you are a new creation in Christ. What does embracing this promise, this reality, just for today do to how you see yourself? Now imagine that this heart-cleansing divine intervention is happening to everyone you meet, indeed to all creation. How does this revelation color how you see people and circumstances? What if each and every day we began with asking God to cleanse our hearts, and each and every night we thanked God for that mercy, and in between we extended that kind of grace to others?

Questions for Reflection

1. When have you poured your heart out to someone? To God? How did it feel to be that vulnerable and honest? What happened as a result?
2. Do you believe transformation, forgiveness, a new way of being and living is possible for you? For others? For our communities, churches, and world?
3. How does the incarnation of Jesus Christ free you to lay your heart bare to God?

Prayer for the Day

Merciful God, there is nothing we can say or do that you do not already know about us. We hide from you as if you do not already know us completely. We hold back that which we think we ought not acknowledge about ourselves as if we could keep secrets from the One who created and redeemed us. Today, we pour out our heart to you in the sure and certain promise of your mercy and your will to transform. Create in us a clean heart, O God, and put a new and right spirit within us. Forgive and free us so that we can sing your praise. Amen.

Wednesday

Proverbs 3:1–8

Trust in the LORD with all your heart,
and do not rely on your own insight.
Proverbs 3:5

Trusting Heart

Remember God's teaching. Hold fast to loyalty and faith-fulness. Do not rely on your own insight. Following these instructions, according to Proverbs, bolsters our trust in the Lord. The teacher wants the pupils to look to God, not themselves, for guidance and wisdom. Trust the Lord with all your heart. In contrast, question your own think-ing and insight. One of the conundrums we face, though, is how to tell the difference. I had a professor who warned us as seminary students that discerning between the voice of God, the voice of Satan, and our own could prove to be a difficult task. Often we want God's stamp of approval on our own judgments and plans so much that we convince ourselves they are synonymous. I appreciate that Anne Lamott quote, "You can safely assume you've created

God in your own image when it turns out that God hates all the same people you do."* Hence the admonishment to trust the Lord with all our heart and not rely on our own insights.

God does not leave us bereft of tools with which to know God's heart, God's will, God's ways. God gifts us with no less than the Word made flesh, those teachings embodied and the kingdom very near, Immanuel, God with us. When we need to check our insights against those of our God we need only look to Jesus to see if one resembles the other. If the likeness between our thinking and that of the teaching of Jesus closely matches, then hold fast to it. If not, be faithful enough to back up, regroup, and think again.

Our culture dissuades us from admitting we might be wrong or even that we are uncertain. Changing our mind on an issue brings forth calls of hypocrisy or weakness or disloyalty. This text reminds us, however, that our only unchanging loyalty is to the Lord and that complete trust in and love of God provides the true north of our wisdom, judgment, and behavior. Trust in the Lord with all your heart and do not rely on your own insight.

In this season of Christmas, the gift of God's Son grants us an unprecedented window into the wisdom, will, and way of the holy. The wisdom of God often deemed foolishness by much of the world. The teachings of Jesus rejected by many. Turn the other cheek. Become like children. Love your enemies. Pray for those who persecute you. The last will be first. I do not believe I would come to these conclusions through my own insights. Instead I am inclined to capitulate to earthly powers, look out for

*Anne Lamott, *Bird by Bird: Some Instructions on Writing and Life*, 2nd ed. (New York: Anchor Books, 1995), 21.

number one, and relish when those I dislike get what I think should be coming to them. No wonder Proverbs tells us to trust in the Lord with all our heart and do not rely on our own insight. When I hold up my conclusions and compare them to the person of Jesus Christ and the teachings of God, the contrast between the two is stark and easy to distinguish after all.

Questions for Reflection

1. How do you remain loyal and faithful to God? How do you "bind them around your neck and write them on the tablet of your heart"?
2. Do you find it difficult to discern God's wisdom from your own? How do you go about telling the difference between the two?
3. Often we are told to "trust your gut." How does that cultural admonishment fit or not with these instructions from Proverbs?

Prayer for the Day

Lord God, you do not leave us to guess your ways and wisdom, but rather provide us with clear commandments, repeated teaching, and your embodied Word, Jesus Christ. We have no excuse for failing to be loyal to your will. Nonetheless, we try to make your teachings match our desires instead of the other way around. Forgive our stubbornness and help us to look to Immanuel, God with us, to learn how you want us to live. Give us the courage to be faithful to you and you alone. Help us to trust in you with all our heart and not rely on our own insight. May we acknowledge you in all our ways so that we do not lose our way. Amen.

Thursday

Matthew 5:1–11

"Blessed are the pure in heart, for they will see God."
Matthew 5:8

Pure Heart

"Pure" is not a word I use with regularity. It seems old fashioned or associated with sexuality, particularly women's sexuality and the need to control it. Purity is equated with chastity in the case of things like "purity rings," but Jesus in the Beatitudes means something much more expansive than refraining from sex before marriage. Perhaps inserting a synonym for "pure" could help to better interpret Jesus' blessing from the Sermon on the Mount. What about, "clean"? "Blessed are the clean in heart, for they will see God." Or how about, "innocent"? "Blessed are the innocent of heart, for they will see God." A little more cumbersome, but still an accurate translation, "void of evil" could work. "Blessed are those void of evil in heart, for they will see God." Blessed are the guiltless, the sincere in heart, for they will see God. Do any of these resonate or relate to how we might seek to set our hearts, our desires, our affections, and impulses so that we might see God?

Those who will see God manage to align their affections and desires with those of the holy. They sincerely seek to act out of a divine impulse devoid of evil. The word that comes to mind is integrity, an alignment of professed belief and real-life actions, a knowledge of moral framework from which decisions and words are constructed and made manifest in the world. Purity of heart does not connote a clueless innocence so much as a stalwart commitment to acting with integrity no matter the cost. Interestingly, the verb "see" in this passage gets translated as "appear" in other New Testament texts. For example, in the transfiguration stories, Moses and Elijah appear with Jesus and those disciples on the mountain get a glimpse of this holy happening. In Luke 1, as Zechariah goes about his priestly duties, an angel of the Lord appears to him, sharing the message that his prayer has been heard and Elizabeth will bear a son, one John the Baptist. It would seem that it is in going about faithfully serving, in seeking to follow, that God appears and is unquestionably seen.

Blessed are those who fulfill the daily duties of discipleship, for God will appear to them as they do so. Blessed are those who attempt to do what is right, regardless of the pressure to do otherwise, for in so doing God shows up. Blessed are those who live with integrity, even when no one is looking, for God sees and will be seen as a result. Having a pure heart, one free of evil, innocent and guiltless, feels impossible. None of us will ever or always be so clean. That, of course, is why we need Jesus, his incarnation, his ministry, his death and resurrection. God creates in us a clean heart, through the gift of the only Son. We can, however, prayerfully, humbly, daily seek to align our heart's desires with that of the One just born in a stable. We can go where he goes: to children, graveyards, and lost sheep. We can sit at table with him as he eats with sinners (of which we are included). We can heed his teachings to wash feet and feed the flock. We can ask the Spirit to show us how to live in ways that reveal the heart of God to the world and when we do, God appears, often in the faces of those right in front of us.

Questions for Reflection

1. What comes to your mind when you hear the word "pure"? Are there other related words that might help you understand Jesus' statement?
2. Can you think of anyone you would characterize as having a pure heart? What about them makes you characterize them as pure-hearted?
3. When have you seen God? How did God appear? What were you doing when you had this encounter?

Prayer for the Day

Lord, we cannot be pure-hearted without your intervention, your teachings, your Spirit. Create in us a clean heart and put a right spirit within us so that our desires align with your will. As we celebrate the birth of our Savior, we look to imitate him, following him wherever he goes, whether to the homes of tax collectors or religious leaders, children or those long suffering with illness, up the mountain or to Jerusalem. As we seek to follow, we trust we will see and recognize you. When you appear to us, may we respond with thanks and praise, rejoicing in your near presence. Amen.

Friday

Matthew 9:2–8

And just then some people were carrying a paralyzed man lying on a bed. When Jesus saw their faith, he said to the paralytic, "Take heart, son; your sins are forgiven."
Matthew 9:2

Take Heart

"Take heart," Jesus says to the man lying on the bed. "Take heart, son; your sins are forgiven." Jesus names this person "son" and proclaims his sins forgiven. This story of a miracle healing gives us no sense of the healed person's reaction to the strange chain of events that get him to the feet of Jesus and result in his ability to walk home. When I read about this exchange, I wonder what the person on the mat thought when Jesus forgave his sins. Did he want his sins forgiven? Was his sin his most pressing concern given all the other obstacles he faced that day? I understand that at that time (and even still sometimes today) people assumed that sickness came tied to sin, a punishment perhaps for the afflicted person's sin or that of those around him. But in that moment of pronouncement did the man on the mat imagine that the natural trajectory of this forgiveness would be freedom from paralysis?

When we find ourselves unable to move, stuck and unable to get ourselves to the feet of Jesus, do we connect God's forgiveness with the ability to get moving again? Can our knowledge of being freed from sin, made new creations in Christ, allow us to take heart and get back on our feet?

I wonder when the time comes and I am utterly dependent upon others for my care, and this time comes for most of us, will I be able to take heart in knowing that I belong to God and am through Jesus Christ irrevocably forgiven and saved? When Jesus tells this person to take heart, he tells each one of us in that moment that we too are God's own and that no infirmity, limitation, or vulnerability will separate us from the love of God. Be healed of whatever prevents you from moving forward in this one, tumultuous, beautiful life. This kind of wholeness encompasses our entire selves and is not contingent upon our physical abilities or lack thereof.

Take heart, if your regrets weigh on you, child of God, you are forgiven. Get up and go in faith to extend mercy to others. Take heart, if you fear you cannot endure one more moment of running through the "what-ifs" in your mind, child of God, the Spirit works through all our choices, missteps, and outright mistakes. Set down the things you cannot change and know that right now God is doing a new thing, with you, through you. Take heart if you cannot get yourself to the feet of Jesus: Immanuel is with you wherever you are, and Christ prays for you even when you lack the faith to pray to him. Take heart, child of God, you are not on this journey alone. The communion of the saints surrounds you, the Spirit intercedes for you, Jesus Christ forgives you, and the love of God will find you, even, especially, when you cannot seek the Lord yourself. Take heart.

Questions for Reflection

1. Has anyone ever intervened on your behalf and gotten you the help you needed but could not get for yourself?
2. When have you carried someone to Jesus when they were in need of healing and help?
3. When you hear Jesus say to you, "Take heart" what do you most need from him in order to do so?

Prayer for the Day

God of healing and wholeness, forgiveness and new life, there are times and circumstances that render us paralyzed, unable to seek you out, utterly dependent upon the kindness of others and the grace of God. While we do not like to feel so helpless, we take heart in knowing that nothing can separate us from your love. We rest in your presence, unsure of what we most need, but confident you know what is best for us and will not hesitate to provide that which will bring grace and mercy to us and through us, to others. We hear with joy your words, "Take heart, child of God, your sins are forgiven." Amen.

Saturday

John 14:1–7

"Do not let your hearts be troubled. Believe in God, believe also in me."

John 14:1

Troubled Heart

Homesickness occupies a unique space in the heart. Missing home blends a longing for the familiar with a need for belonging, for being known, loved, and accepted. Homesickness perhaps employs selective memory, highlighting that which is good and muting that which is troubling in our home life. When one of my children, away from home for the first time, told me she missed my cooking, I knew that homesickness entails a strange yearning for place and people that includes those quirky, less-than-perfect aspects of living in community. Even when our home life is complicated (and whose family is not complicated?), we often want to return to it when circumstances take us away. In this text from John, Jesus assures his anxious disciples that he will not leave them forever, that he will bring them to himself, eventually, and that he prepares a place for them.

Our hearts grow troubled when we lack a place that welcomes us, a space where we can be less than our best selves. Without a place of refuge and respite, we become exhausted, fearful and, well, troubled. Questions about our worth and lovability and value swirl when we cannot find a space of acceptance, a place where we are celebrated despite our mistakes and missteps. Jesus, in this pastoral conversation with his closest friends, on the cusp of the end of his earthly life, says emphatically that such a space exists, not just in the future heavenly mansion, but right now in him. "I am the way, the truth and the life," Jesus says (v. 6).

That expansive space of exuberant welcome, that place of rest for our souls, of green pastures and living water, has been prepared for us by no less than Jesus Christ himself. There is indeed nowhere we can flee to or be exiled away from the God who loves us. And yet, like Thomas, we often ask, "Lord, how can we know the way?" Often, we feel unmoored, at loose ends, our hearts troubled and our souls restless. When we experience that deep, existential homesickness, how do we find our way? Perhaps we begin with remembering where we have been and how we have gotten this far.

We remember being fed with unexpected bread and called to journey alongside unexpected people. We recall the times that threatening storms did not overtake us and strangers opened their homes to us. We think back on all the wilderness places in which we were sustained, what we learned and who walked with us when we thought we could not keep going, and how God brought us to safety. We believe that Jesus, true to his promises, prepares a place for us, and will somehow make a way for us when we are flummoxed about which direction to go. As I reminded that homesick child, you are not alone, we will not abandon you, you are loved and lovable, and soon we will be together again. Let not your heart be troubled, and if it is, call on those of us who will remind you of these truths until you believe them without a doubt.

Questions for Reflection

1. When have you had a troubled heart? What made it so? How do you ease that trouble?
2. When have you felt like you lost your way, or did not know the way? Who helped you?
3. What does it mean for you that Jesus is the way, the truth, and the life? That Jesus prepares a place for you and will bring you to himself?

Prayer for the Day

Lord Christ, your promises of place and peace, of truth and direction, of life and mercy, uphold us when we feel lost and troubled. We yearn to be with you and know that if we follow you, we will find home. When anxiety overwhelms us and we wonder if we belong, remind us again of how far we have come, of all the times and ways you have provided abundantly for us. Send others to walk alongside us and send us to the lost and lonely so that all of us will know the love of God you came to show the world. Amen.

Second Week of Christmas

Gold

Sunday

1 Corinthians 3:1–15

Now if anyone builds on the foundation with gold, silver, precious stones, wood, hay, straw—the work of each builder will become visible, for the Day will disclose it, because it will be revealed with fire, and the fire will test what sort of work each has done.

1 Corinthians 3:12–13

Gold Foundations

Divisions in the church prompt Paul to write to the Christians of Corinth. People in the community choose sides, affiliate with different leaders, line up in favor or against various practices. Their conflict escalates to the point of jeopardizing their witness to Jesus Christ and tearing their nascent community apart. People, then and now, give into the temptation of tribalism. People perpetually draw lines between each other and villainize those on the other side of their humanly created walls. Paul reminds Christians of the need to focus on the One in whom they are united: Jesus Christ.

139

We are God's servants, Paul tells the Corinthians. God gives the growth, no matter who plants or who waters. He then switches metaphors and calls Christians, calls us, God's building. Disciples of Jesus Christ become the spaces, places, and structures that reflect the character and will of the God who creates and calls us. Just as the sacraments, the water, bread and wine, are outward signs of invisible grace, we disciples, through God's grace, are manifestations of grace to the world, outposts of mercy, hostels of hospitality, lodges of love, high rises of justice. Such structures can only stand, however, if they are erected on solid foundations. These kinds of buildings can only weather storms and the test of time if they stand on sound, strong, foundations.

Paul asks the Corinthians to consider what it is they stand on and subsequently stand for in this life. All will be revealed in due time, those inner workings, the framing and foundation of our lives, God knows and others will see as time and challenges weather our surfaces. When we face challenges, when we are tempted to capitulate to cultural definitions of identity, when we feel threatened by outsized circumstances like pandemics, natural disasters, or economic hardships, what will be revealed about what matters most to us, what we stand for, and who we stand with?

Even gold, given enough pressure and heat, will give way, never mind straw or sand. The chief cornerstone the builders reject, Jesus Christ, is the only foundation upon which to build a structure that will reflect our Creator, Paul admonishes those bickering Corinthians. Our servant Lord, the carpenter from Nazareth, whose tools consisted of radical welcome, amazing grace, compassion, justice, peace, mercy, and—most of all—sacrificial love, prepares a place for us and sends us to make our lives and our communities buildings of hope, joy, and love, too. Structures with these foundations stand for Jesus and bear witness to the unifying, forgiving, reconciling, restorative power of the master builder we follow. When it comes down to it, what is the rock bottom foundation of our lives and what will be constructed as a result?

Questions for Reflection

1. What is foundational for you? What do you build your life on and around? How is that evident in your living? Your priorities?
2. Paul uses two metaphors in this text. He says we are God's field and God's building. Which of these metaphors resonates with you and why?
3. What, when tests and challenges come our way, is revealed about our foundations and framework? What do we stand for and what holds us up?

Prayer for the Day

Lord Christ, when we build our lives upon you, structuring our priorities in light of your call and your character, we create communities that glorify God and reflect your saving love. Too often we give into the temptation to construct a world out of lesser materials, flimsy values, shiny objects that distract and disintegrate under even a little pressure. Quality construction, the craft of discipleship, takes patience, a commitment to being your apprentice, and daily practice. In a culture that craves instant gratification, help us to remember the value of integrity and the joy of participating in your ever-forming-and-being-formed creation. Amen.

Monday

James 5:1–6

Your gold and silver have rusted, and their rust will be
evidence against you, and it will eat your flesh like fire. You
have laid up treasure for the last days.

James 5:3

Corroded Gold

James, that short book of the New Testament akin to the
person in the meeting or the family who refuses to use
civil norms, read the room, or be socially appropriate.
Could James not tone it down a bit? Lighten up on all
the judgment? Let us enjoy some polite conversation and
perhaps stop offending people left and right? Apparently
not. James admonishes us about our speech, making sure
we know that our words matter and ought to be consistent
with both the content and character of the Word made
flesh. James tells us bluntly to jettison cultural categories
of value and show no partiality between people. Further,
we get this jeremiad in chapter 5 regarding wealth. James

cares not at all about being liked. His litmus test is the truth of the gospel, offensive or not.

Rusted gold and silver indicates that the one who possesses it did not steward it in a manner pleasing to God. Rusted gold reveals that resources were hoarded or buried, not distributed and shared. No bigger barns allowed for disciples of the One who instructed his followers to take nothing for their journey. No burying talents to followers of the servant Lord who risked it all in order to save the world. Rusted gold is wasted gold, so far as James and the gospel are concerned. Rusted gold shows that the owner stored up treasures on earth, forgetting where true value lies. Even worse, that rusted treasure should have been given as wages to those who labored in the fields. That rusty gold represents stolen goods, robbed from those who earned it and needed it to live.

James does not mince words or lack clarity. But what of those who read this passage and think we are off the hook if we lack a treasure trove of riches or feel confident we are not withholding anyone's wages? Can we just cheer James's rant on or is this a cautionary tale for all of us, not just those in the upper 2 percent? Make no mistake, James is not speaking metaphorically here, he really wants Christians to know that nothing is off-limits to God's claim on our lives and our money should be used in ways that reflect our loyalty to God. Nonetheless, no matter where we fall on the economic ladder, James' word about gold and silver applies to us. James reminds us of Jesus' call that those with two coats are called to give one away because those with no coats are more valuable in God's sight than any amount of gold.

Painful and graphic as these verses sound, they offer a profound and hopeful truth: We are not the sum of our gold. No matter how much our world scrambles to accumulate wealth, no matter how much culture demonizes the poor, the gospel truth declares that human beings, created by God and called good, matter in and of themselves, regardless of their earthly status. Imagine if we built our society around that gospel truth? Picture a community, a country, a world where the first concern, the litmus test for policy and practice, was not profit, but people—all people. Imagine if we kept these verses from James ever before us and used them as a cipher to discern how we used our resources and what we truly value. For profit prisons could not exist using this rubric. The wealth and opportunity gap would disappear. We would be not only good neighbors, we would create, cultivate, and sustain good neighborhoods.

James reiterates Jesus' truth: Where your treasure is, there your heart is also. Rusted gold is undeniable evidence that we do not love who or what we say we do.

Questions for Reflection

1. What is your reaction to these verses? Where do you place yourself? As the rich person or the laborer?
2. How does this passage apply not only to individuals but also to entire societies?
3. Even if we are not accumulating vast quantities of gold, how do we participate in structures that oppress workers? What are we called to do to address economic disparities and exploitation?

Prayer for the Day

Servant Lord, you came not as a person of wealth and high status, but were born in a stable to a humble family. Your disciples did not represent the top of the social ladder. You went to those on the margins and proclaimed good news to the poor. When we are tempted to hear the siren call of wealth and status, call us back to you. When we give in to idolatry and greed, send your Spirit to reorder our priorities and align our living with your commandments. When we judge ourselves and others by earthly standards, remind us that our irrevocable and incalculable worth is found in you. Amen.

Tuesday

Genesis 41:37–45

Removing his signet ring from his hand, Pharaoh put it on Joseph's hand; he arrayed him in garments of fine linen, and put a gold chain around his neck.

Genesis 41:42

Pharaoh's Gold

Joseph, draped in the symbols of Pharaoh's empire, receives authority over all of Egypt. Pharaoh gives Joseph a new name, even. Joseph appears fully co-opted into this regime. The story calls to mind others in Scripture where people get renamed and appointed to a particular role or work. Abram becomes Abraham, Sarai renamed Sarah, their new names representing their new call as the parents of many nations. The angel and then God tell Jacob he will be Israel. Jesus tells Simon he will now be known as Peter, the rock upon which Jesus will build his church.

Renaming and transformation, signs and symbols of a person's role, office, or vocation, such rituals get repeated in the biblical narrative. Priests are anointed with oil and wear particular clothing. The water of baptism marks a change in life and loyalties. Those new converts to Christianity hand over their gold for the good of the community. But here we have Joseph taking on the Pharaoh's gold and being given a new identity in service to the earthly leader, not the Lord of heaven and earth. What do we make of what could be seen as a misordering of priorities? Is not Joseph to retain his Jewishness at any cost (like Shadrach, Meshach, and Abednego will) instead of don the gold chain and signet ring of empire?

What is our relationship to political authorities? What is our role in relationship to earthly powers? What outward symbols of empire should we shun and when is it all right to wear them without shame? A long-standing debate within Christianity involves the role of the church and believers in social issues. Often Christians remained stalwart in the notion that only spiritual matters mattered. No need to get involved in the messy machinations of worldly debates, focus solely on the soul. But this story of Joseph decked in Pharaoh's gold tells an entirely different story. God uses Joseph, totally embedded in the world of the most powerful leader on earth at the time, to further salvation history. Joseph, called *Zaphenath-paneah* by the Egyptians, will be God's instrument for saving God's people. God uses the renamed-by-Pharaoh Joseph to prevent the starvation of the Israelites. God cares about not only spiritual things, but our bodily well-being too. God uses even Pharaoh's gold for good.

Nothing in all creation is off-limits for God's use. The challenge for us remains discernment. While Joseph's role within the empire, his dripping in gold that represents Pharaoh, ultimately allows him to save not only his brothers who threw him in the pit, but his aging father and the Israelite people from whom Jesus will come.

Sometimes, clearly, those of us whose ultimate loyalty is to the Triune God are called to work within earthly power structures in ways that further God's plans, in ways that reveal God's will, but we must do so ever mindful of the temptation to make acquiring and keeping Pharaoh's gold and status our goal. We may work within earthly empires, but never for them. No matter whose signet ring we wear, we belong to God.

Questions for Reflection

1. Can you think of other stories in the Bible when someone is given a new name? What is the context and what changes as a result of this new name?
2. What are the outward signs and symbols you wear and what do they represent? A gold wedding ring? T-shirts with sports teams emblazoned upon them?
3. How do we work within earthly powers without capitulating to working for them?

Prayer for the Day

Almighty God, Lord of all, Alpha and Omega, your sovereignty is over everything seen and unseen. Nothing is off-limits to your providence and power. When we are called to work within earthly powers, keep us always, ultimately, working for you. When we are tempted to want more gold, greater status, the trappings of worldly adulation, interrupt that endless and empty quest and call us back to you. May all we do, wherever we are called to do it, whatever outward symbols we don, all point to the love of the One we ultimately follow, our Savior Jesus Christ. Amen.

Wednesday

Exodus 32:1–6

[Aaron] took the gold from them, formed it in a mold, and cast an image of a calf; and they said, "These are your gods, O Israel, who brought you up out of the land of Egypt!"
Exodus 32:4

Idol of Gold

The Israelites get anxious due to Moses' delayed return. Aaron takes on their anxiety and devises a plan to defuse it. To be fair, the people asked Aaron to create gods for them. He did not come up with the idea, he simply caved to the pressure and put the scheme in motion. The fearful people participate willingly, eagerly even, turning over their gold, that precious commodity, to be formed into the calf that they will worship. When anxiety swells and uncertainty persists, human beings will do a lot to mitigate their stress, even temporarily.

While we may not form farm animals out of our jewelry, we no less find less than helpful ways to ease our apprehensions. We lash out at those closest to us. We self-medicate. We triangulate. We scapegoat and blame. We sabotage relationships. We distract ourselves with things or distance ourselves from those who might tell us truths we do not want to hear. This story is, of course, about idolatry, but it is also a story about trauma and pain. Yes, the narrative of the golden calf provides us with a cautionary tale about the dangers of worshiping false gods of our own making, but it also reminds us to pay attention to what we do when we, and the systems, institutions, and communities we inhabit, are under duress.

I sympathize with the people who come to Aaron seeking relief and some sense of security and something upon which to focus other than their deepest fears. I feel for Aaron trying to lead in the middle of an unprecedented crisis with no sense of when the person who put him in charge will return. When we create false gods, when we turn over our resources to endeavors that cannot satisfy, that are inert and impotent, that waste our energy and fail to deliver on their promises, could we instead pour out our grief to the God who freed us from Pharaoh and is right now making a way for us in the wilderness?

In seasons of upheaval and hurt, people demand relief, in whatever form they can find. The challenge for those in leadership is to remain nonanxious, connected to but not co-opted by those clamoring for a golden calf. Lament may well be in order. Name the pain and weep with those who weep. Recognize where that idolatrous urge comes from and rather than give in to it, address the root cause. Instead of using energy and resources for a false god, recognize the grief and know God sees the hurt of God's people and will respond with compassion. Remember all God has done to get the Israelites to this point and all God will do to bring them to the promised land. Moses' absence will not last forever and God's promises can be trusted. When we grow anxious, rather than ask Aaron for a golden calf, we can call on the God who created us and know our cries will be heard.

Questions for Reflection

1. What do you do when you get anxious? How do you seek relief? How would you like to react to stressful situations and seasons?
2. What form does the golden calf take in your life? Your community? Our culture?
3. Where are you putting your gold, investing your energy and resources?

Prayer for the Day

Gracious God, you send your Son to reveal your boundless love for us. You yearn to be in relationship with us even when we turn our backs on you. You tell us to not be afraid, to not be anxious, to trust your presence and providence. Yet, we give in to our unease and act in ways that hurt ourselves and others. Even then your mercy persists. You do not abandon us. You forgive us. Your compassion pursues us. You make a way for us when we see no way. You provide rest for our souls and relief for our fear. We give thanks for your grace and worship you alone. Amen.

Thursday

Psalm 19

More to be desired are they than gold,
even much fine gold;
sweeter also than honey,
and drippings of the honeycomb.
Psalm 19:10

More Precious than Gold

Psalm 19 sings of God's glory. The heavens, the night, all creation tells of God's grandeur and beauty. Everywhere the psalmist looks, God's loveliness and goodness is revealed. The epitome of that divine perfection becomes evident in God's law. God's law revives the soul. God's law causes those who abide by it to rejoice. It grants wisdom, certainty, enlightenment, and righteousness. Psalm 19 exudes a love for God and God's commandments, reminding us of the preciousness of our relationship with God.

More than gold, fine gold, should we desire the law, ordinances, and commandments of God. These holy gifts provide boundaries that create human spaces that reflect divine glory and wisdom. They mold human lives into clearer images of our divine maker. Further, they enable rejoicing and refreshment, even repair. For those of us celebrating the birth of Jesus Christ, reveling in God's law may not be on the top of our to-do list. We focus on the person of Jesus Christ, remembering the stories of his birth, perhaps hearing the soaring language of John's Gospel about grace upon grace. But Psalm 19 reminds us of the law Jesus came not to abolish but to fulfill. The psalmist sings with the communion of the saints of God's creative power, God's relentless will to be in relationship with us, God's desire to not only bring us into being but give us all we need for abundant life, together. More than gold, fine gold, should we yearn to exist within the beautiful constraints of God's law. When we seek to love the Lord our God with all our heart, soul, mind, and strength, and our neighbors as ourselves, we not only fulfill the greatest commandment and the one like it, we return to our creator and discover the relief of letting go of so much else that weighs us down and impedes the joy of self and others.

Imagine, for a moment, recognizing God's glory in everything: every person, that beam of light coming through the trees, the caw of the crow on the street light in the strip mall parking lot, the dew on the grass, the patterns of clouds in the sky. Imagine that recognition calling forth a knowledge of God's power and God's goodness that does not create the world and leave it to its own devices, but continues to make all things new, sending even the Son to show us who and whose we are. So invested in the cosmos is our Lord that God articulates how we might fully experience beauty, goodness, truth, rightness, repair. God gives us the law and then sends the Son to fulfill it, and now we see God's glory, full of grace and truth. Grace and truth, the Word made flesh, more to be desired than any gold, sweeter than honey. Imagine how the world might look when the words of our mouths and the meditations of our hearts embody that grace and truth too. I picture rejoicing and enlightenment, revival and righteousness, communities that know that love for one another is far more precious than any amount of the finest gold.

Questions for Reflection

1. When have you been struck by God's glory? What elicited this revelation?
2. Do you ever think about the gift of God's law—God's commandments and ordinances? Why are such instructions a gift to us?
3. What do you find yourself desiring, wanting? Do these yearnings reflect God's law or not?

Prayer for the Day

More to be desired than any material resources, any worldly goods, a relationship with you is what we truly want, Lord God. We know that you yearn for us to be in right relationship with you, with each other, with creation. You tell us what is required and you show us in the person of your Son, our Savior, Jesus Christ, how we should live in your beloved world. When the meditations of our hearts and the speech from our mouths resound with the Word made flesh, we echo your glory, goodness, beauty, truth, and grace. Make of us not only followers of your law, but conduits of your commanded, lovely, reviving, joyous love. Amen.

Friday

Exodus 35:20–29

So they came, both men and women; all who were of a willing heart brought brooches and earrings and signet rings and pendants, all sorts of gold objects, everyone bringing an offering of gold to the LORD.

Exodus 35:22

Gold Offerings

The building of the tabernacle gets under way, despite the murmuring in the desert, the idolatry of the golden calf, all the conflict and pain, the people undertake the construction of a sacred space in which to worship the God who refuses to give up on them. Exodus 35:21 reads, "And they came, everyone whose heart was stirred, and everyone whose spirit was willing, and brought the LORD's offering to be used for the tent of meeting, and for all its service, and for the sacred vestments." The unqualified nature of this statement moves me every time I read it: And they came, hearts stirred, spirit willing, and gave something to be used for the tent of meeting and the services that would take place within it. No coercion. No cajoling. No slick marketing campaign or incentives needed. God's people felt compelled to contribute to that which would enable them to gather and worship.

When was the last time you were so moved, so stirred and willing to offer something precious to you for the sake of something larger than yourself? One gets the sense that those who had escaped Egypt and trekked through the desert could not be held back from showing their joy in tangible ways that day they brought forth the gold treasures so important they grabbed them as they made that dangerous dash just ahead of Pharaoh's army. There are times when nothing can prevent people from joyously sharing their resources, the occasion, the emotions stir hearts and make the spirit willing, more than willing, to contribute. This scene brings to mind the account of the feeding of the 5,000 in John's Gospel. The boy with five barley loaves of bread and two fish, heart stirred perhaps, spirit obviously willing, gives his lunch to Jesus for the impromptu meeting and the communion that will ensue.

Such unstoppable, exuberant giving marks the lives of those whose hearts are stirred by the love of the God who saves them. Sometimes this takes the form of giving gold, other times the generosity comes in the form of hospitality, compassion, or encouragement. Encountering this kind of unmitigated outpouring of self, not out of obligation or guilt, expectation or righteousness, but solely from a moved heart and spirit, elicits joy from others.

I have worked in the nonprofit world most of my working life and often it felt as if much of my time was spent asking for the resources to enable the mission. What letter, strategy, medium, technique would be effective? Articulating the vision and impact of the work mattered, to be sure, but one of the most moving gifts received came unbidden. I received an email informing me of a check in the mail from a person whose stirred heart led to the offering. No strings attached. The giver, in gratitude for all God's goodness to her, felt moved to support those engaged in what she deemed meaningful mission that helped others. I engaged in correspondence with this person and even through email, her joy and exuberance was evident. She took delight in offering her gold, yes, but also in the flowers in her front yard, her daily activities, and in her community. The gold she gave helped our mission, the place from which she gave it inspired us to fulfill that mission in ways that reflected her joy in supporting it.

Questions for Reflection

1. When has your heart been stirred to give? What moved you to make that offering?
2. When have you been on the receiving end of an offering made from a place of joy?
3. What prevents us from being moved to give of ourselves? Our resources?

Prayer for the Day

God of grace, you bring us through the darkest valleys and the most dangerous of wilderness places. When we get to a place of rest, we cannot help but rejoice and give you thanks. Our hearts are stirred and our spirits moved to show you our gratitude in tangible ways. We want to offer you not only our gold, but our entire selves. We come together in order to praise you, worship you and revel in the recognition that you heard our cries and saved us. Receive our gifts, bless and use them for the services in the tent of meeting and the building of your kingdom on earth. Amen.

Saturday

Matthew 2:2–12

On entering the house, they saw the child with Mary his mother; and they knelt down and paid him homage. Then, opening their treasure chests, they offered him gifts of gold, frankincense, and myrrh.

Matthew 2:11

Gift of Gold

What would an infant need with gold? With frankincense or myrrh, for that matter? The symbolism of the frankincense and myrrh points to the burial of Jesus even at his birth. Both were used for sacred purposes, burned in the temple, used for anointing. Clearly, the three magi understood that this baby was special, and all three elements were valuable, expensive. But what of the gift of gold, what does it represent? It seems like the offering that does not belong. Certainly, gold befits kings. Royal persons adorn themselves with it, put it on their palaces. However, gold holds no medicinal qualities, does not smell fragrant or quell pain. Gold equals money, currency.

While frankincense and myrrh symbolized Jesus' divinity, his sacredness, his saving death to come, gold represents his humanity, the truth that this Messiah will know the trials and tribulations of work, earthly economics, and all the vicissitudes of human finitude. Like it or not, gold, or lack thereof, impacts people's well-being greatly. I wonder if Mary and Joseph saw the gift of gold and let out a sigh of relief. Perhaps they thought they could tuck it away, like a savings bond or the seeds of a college fund, a small bit of security to be used if times got really tough. Maybe Mary and Joseph appreciated the valuable, but less than practical, frankincense and myrrh, unsure what at that point such gifts meant, but knew that the gold could come in handy in real, material, bread-on-the-table terms.

This magi's gift of gold reminds us that the Holy Family was a real family, not unlike real families we know, attempting to raise children while working, imparting values, cooking meals, shaping character, and getting tired. In all the angel appearances and voices from heaven and strange star sightings, sometimes we neglect to emphasize the miracle of incarnation, the truth that the Son of God becomes enfleshed as a real baby reared by real parents, parents who must figure out daily living in an often threatening, scary, uncertain world. Just like parents today. Just like us. The gift of gold reminds us of these realities and the truth that Jesus is fully divine and fully human.

I am grateful for that magi's most practical of gifts: money. That magi's offering tethers Jesus to the messiness of making a living. That magi's gift renders it impossible for me to imagine that Jesus, and Mary, and Joseph, did not struggle with the daily frustrations and pains everyday people, all people confront. In the book of Flannery O'Connor's essays, *Mystery and Manners*, O'Connor writes, "When the physical fact is separated from the spiritual reality, the dissolution of belief is eventually inevitable."* More than any of the three gifts, the magi who brought the gold tied the secular, everyday needs of early life to the sacred incarnation of our saving God. Our human concerns, joys, and troubles, with the Word made flesh, made the spiritual and the physical inseparable. Thanks be to God, even gold is not off-limits to God's grace.

Questions for Reflection

1. If you were to bring a gift to the infant Jesus, what would it be and why?
2. Do you imagine that there are areas of our life that are off-limits to God's grace, guidance, use?
3. When do we attempt to separate spiritual and physical realities? Why do we want to put the spiritual and physical in different, separate categories?

Prayer for the Day

Lord Christ, we bring the gift of ourselves and offer it totally to you. You took on our humanity, in all its messiness and pain, its finitude and struggle. As a result, nothing and no one is off-limits to your saving love. When we want to wall off places in our lives or hold back anything from your transforming grace, remind us that you came to save sinners and will not reject any aspect of us, not even those we most fear you or others will reject. We rejoice that whatever we offer you in faith, you take, bless, break, and use to multiply mercy for all. Amen.

---

*Flannery O'Connor, *Mystery and Manners: Occasional Prose*, ed. Sally and Robert Fitzgerald (New York: Farrar, Straus & Giroux, 1969) 161–62.

Epiphany: Stars

Matthew 2:1–6

*In the time of King Herod, after Jesus was born in
Bethlehem of Judea, wise men from the East came to
Jerusalem, asking, "Where is the child who has been born
king of the Jews? For we observed his star at its rising, and
have come to pay him homage."*

Matthew 2:1–2

Stars in the Dark

Noticing stars, for most of us, requires intentionality.
Stars, after all, cannot be seen during the day, get obscured
by light pollution, and exist far above our heads. To see
stars, in the literal sense, we must go out into the dark
and look up. Neither of these acts come naturally to me.
When I happen to be out at night, I seek lighted paths,
not spaces conducive to stargazing. I make a point not
to linger in the dark, employing my cell phone flashlight
and looking directly in front of me instead. When outside
in the dark, I want to get inside to the light as quickly
as possible. And yet, Epiphany reminds us that it is in

dwelling in deep darkness and looking up into the vastness of space that we find the star that leads us to Jesus.
Finding Jesus calls on us to stay in places we otherwise
would not remain and cast our gaze beyond the few feet
ahead of us.

Epiphany calls on us to think and act expansively and
with trust, to consider not only our immediate circumstances and circles of concern, but the whole of creation that Jesus came to redeem. The practice of "star"
words has gained popularity. A word is randomly given
to church goers and that "star word" is to guide them
throughout the year. "Grace" or "witness" or "patience"
or "peace." I hear from those who participate in this new
ritual how meaningful this practice can be as their word
helps them focus or stay grounded. I think anything that
helps us focus on Jesus and stay grounded in the gospel is
arguably a good thing. My hope is that anything affiliated
with Epiphany helps us go out into the dark and look up,
to expand our purview and our risk-taking for Christ.

I find it all too easy to stay in the confines of known
environments and concern myself solely with my own
worries and those in my immediate circles. The coming
of the three kings from far-away places, those who pil-
grimage long distances in the dark, looking up and following a star, prevents those of us who follow Jesus from
remaining safe and living small.

In elementary school my family moved from a bus-
tling Canadian city to the rural American South. At first,
the change in the soundtrack arrested me. Cicadas and
tree frogs replaced sirens and car horns. Sleep evaded me
those first few weeks in my new bedroom. So much so
that I went to my window to survey my unfamiliar new
neighborhood. That is when I could not help but look up.
The visibility after the sun had long set arrested me. Why

was it so bright at night? My gaze moved skyward and the number and luminosity of the stars was breathtaking. I had never seen anything like it before. The unexpected beauty moved me to get a fuller look and I found myself eager to be out after dark so that I might get a glimpse of this glorious, unexpected sight.

Discovering Jesus, being found by him, moves us to go out and look up, to see beauty where we never noticed it before, to be unafraid to go out into the dark, to expand our horizons in ways that cause us to care for all creation, not only the few feet directly in front of us.

Questions for Reflection
1. When have you struggled to look up and out? What keeps you from venturing out in search of Jesus?
2. When have you been struck by the beauty of the night sky? Do you ever go out and stargaze? If so, what do you think and feel when you see that expanse of space?
3. Where might your search for Jesus take you this year?

Prayer for the Day
Lord of sea and sky, you create the earth and all that is within it, the moon and stars, the sun and clouds, no place is off-limits to your goodness. As we reflect on those who came from far away to find Jesus, we rejoice that we know and worship him. When we get fixated on ourselves and the few feet directly in front of us, move us to go out and look up, to remember you are Lord of all and that when we seek you, we will find you. Amen.

Baptism of the Lord: Water

Mark 1:9–11

And just as [Jesus] was coming up out of the water, he saw the heavens torn apart and the Spirit descending like a dove on him. And a voice came from heaven, "You are my Son, the Beloved; with you I am well pleased."

Mark 1:10–11

Life-Giving Water

I picture Jesus coming up for air, glancing upward, and getting unequivocal affirmation of his identity and call. Still dripping with water, he hears the voice of God claim him, love him, delight in him. Throughout his earthly ministry I suspect Jesus recalled this moment so as to survive the wilderness, persist in proclaiming good news, and remain stalwart in fulfilling the mission he became incarnate to complete. While the ruptured heavens and the descending Spirit may be extraordinary, the water was accessible and a daily necessity. Perhaps God designed baptism for Jesus, for us, to remember that heaven and earth are intimately connected, to know without doubt

that our embodied selves are beloved of God and therefore important.

I would like to think that every time Jesus took a drink
of water or ventured out on a boat or sat by the sea and
preached or went to a well, he remembered his baptism. I
would like to think when he struggled with the disciples'
misunderstandings or grew frustrated with the Pharisee's
hypocrisy, when he simply got tired or wanted to give
up, he drank a cup of water and recalled the voice that
resounded from heaven that day he broke through the
surface of the Jordan River. "You are my Son, the beloved;
with you I am well pleased." Those words of assurance I
hope eased his burden and enabled him to persist in order
that I might some day be named and claimed by God in
the waters of baptism too.

Water, so ordinary, so powerful, so necessary, life-
giving, but potentially life-threatening, an element we
cannot live without, should not take for granted, and
ought to respect. People walk miles to get water, dig
deeper and deeper wells to access it, and find refreshment and fun in playing in it. Water shapes landscapes
and impacts weather. We drink it and bathe in it. Is there
a more versatile compound in all creation? When Jesus
came up out of that river and heaven and earth collided
and the Spirit got let loose in the world, all of our human
finitude and chaos became fodder for Jesus' ministry of
redemption. None of us too dirty, too thirsty, too hard-
ened or too far gone to be off-limits to the baptismal
water that declares our God-given worth and goodness.

Maybe, just maybe, when Jesus encountered water after
that day he came up for air out of the Jordan, he remembered who and whose he was, why he became incarnate
and what he would accomplish for the sake of the world.
Those cups of water given, feet washed, encounters at the

well, storms on the sea, and rain from the sky all became the voice of God to him, the Spirit speaking of the living water he came to be and the living water he would create out of believers' hearts. Living water that would save and heal, slake thirst and clean dirt, provide hope and make life not only possible, but abundant. Maybe remembering this truth with each drop of water he came across kept Jesus going and maybe, if we remember Jesus' baptism and our own, every drop of water can remind us of the intimate, unbreakable connection between heaven and earth, between us and the divine.

Questions for Reflection

1. If you are baptized, what do you know about your baptism? What difference does it make to you that you are baptized?
2. What is your relationship to water? Has water been scarce or abundant in your experience? Do you delight in it or are you fearful of it? How does your experience of water shape your understanding of Jesus saying that he is living water?
3. Could you remember that God claims and loves you every time you encounter water?

Prayer for the Day

Almighty God, you create, sustain, and redeem every corner of the earth, every cell of our being. Nothing and no one is off-limits to your love. When Jesus came up out of the water, you told him who and whose he was. You do no less with us. Such grace is beyond our ability to fully fathom, and yet we rejoice that you delight in us. May we delight in you, daily, and remember with joy that we are yours, we are beloved. Every time we encounter water, may the Spirit speak to us through it, reminding us that we are your children, reflections of you, called good. Amen.

Find digital extras for small-group discussion,
preaching, and worship at
www.wjkbooks.com/AdventInPlainSight.

CPSIA information can be obtained
at www.ICGtesting.com
Printed in the USA
LVHW020704260622
721958LV00007B/7

9 780664 267148